Virginia Colonial Abstracts
Volume #31

I0091024

Lower Norfolk County Virginia

Wills & Deeds

- 1651-1654 -

By:
Beverley Fleet

Southern Historical Press, Inc.
Greenville, South Carolina

Please direct all correspondence and orders to:

www.southernhistoricalpress.com
or
SOUTHERN HISTORICAL PRESS, Inc.
PO BOX 1267
Greenville, SC   29601
southernhistoricalpress@gmail.com

Originally published: Richmond, VA.   1948
Copyright 1948 by: Beverley Fleet
ISBN #0-89308-388-7
All rights Reserved.
Printed in the United States of America

PREFACE

It would be nice to write a dignified and profound preface in regard to the Lower Norfolk records. No. We will have to leave that to the historians if they ever fall that low. Oftentimes what they have to say is quite true. Of course they are not all liars, prostitutes and fools as my old friend Morgan Robinson, and the Englishman, Horace Rounds, used to casually remark. It would be entertaining to hear what these deceased gentlemen (not so gentle) would have to say concerning Toynbee, the prevailing fashion in history. Our good friends the historians love to talk (or write) for the pleasure of hearing themselves talk. A most charming diversion from the dull facts of history.

Upon that premise, those of us who traffic only in originals are also subject to question. The following trivialities in example:

While working upon these Abstracts, an interruption came from a curious and interfereing old jackass. I explained that the Lower Norfolk records were interesting enough - if I could only read them. The reward for this politeness being superior comment about my attempting work beyond my capacity, etc. I thought to myself that it might be lucky not to be so cocksure. In these Abstracts I prefer to remain uncertain. There is some detail you might as well know. In the originals the capital R and the capital K are altogether too much alike. Thus Key may well be Rey (modern Ray), Kay, or even Roy. All four being good Virginia names. You can easily bend the original to suit your own premise, a little trick genealogists have been known to do. Also S and B. Difficult to know which is the son and which is the other, if you understand the indelicate suggestion. As for Francis Laud or Franois Land, I am almost sure it was Land (?).

A map of the Norfolk area will assist in study of these records. The names of Lambert Point and Willoughby Spit have gone to the most remote ports of this earth, while that of Lynhaven has certainly gone to Hell, many young Virginia gentlemen that I knew myself, having all but died of drinking whiskey and eating their oysters on the same spree. One becomes so hungry down there in the salt air, and so thirsty in the intense heat.

                                                           Beverley Fleet

Richmond, Virginia.
1st May 1948.

Lower Norfolk
County Chart.

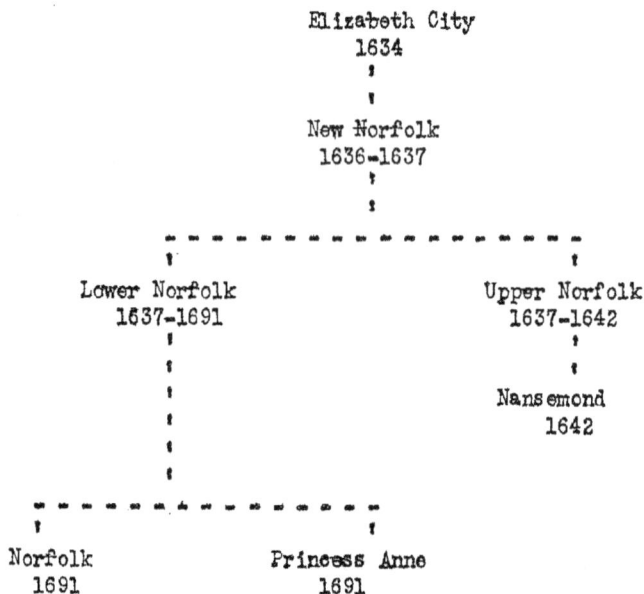

Elizabeth City
1634
:
:
New Norfolk
1636-1637
:
:
- - - - - - - - - - - - - - - - -
:   :
Lower Norfolk   Upper Norfolk
1637-1691   1637-1642
:   :
:   :
:   Nansemond
:   1642
:
:
- - - - - - - - - - - -
:   :
Norfolk   Princess Anne
1691   1691

The above chart is from 'Virginia Counties' by Morgan Poitiaux Robinson.
page 165.
This book is now out of print.

Norfolk County Records.

May be consulted in Archives Division of Virginia State Library,
Richmond, Virginia. Photostat copies - very good.

1646 - 1651   Wills and Deeds B. (VI), index, 211 fo.

1651 - 1656   Wills and Deeds C, (XIII), index, 133 fo. These Abstracts
              are from this volume.

1656 - 1666   Wills and Deeds D. (II), index, 444 pp.

1666 - 1675   Wills and Deeds E. Part 1, Wills and Deeds (V), index,
              188 fo.
              Part II. Orders, 1665 - 1675. 130 fo.

1723 - 1733   Wills, etc. (Contains Orders 1724 1734)
              113 pp. Wills, etc.
              212 pp. Orders.

1836 - 1868   Will Book. No. 6 (XXII), index, 643 pp.

Also:

1675 - 1686   Deed Book, No.4 (XIX), index, 252 fo.

1703 - 1706   Deed Book, No.7. (XI), index, 125 fo.

1708 - 1710   Deed Book, No.8. 164 fo.

1718 - 1719   Deed Book, No. 10. 179 fo.

1730 - 1734   Deed Book, No.11. 172 pp.

1733 - 1739   Deed Book, No. 12, index. 365 pp.

(continued)

Norfolk County Records (continued)

1750 - 1752   Deed Book, No.15. index, 183 fo.

1665 - 1675   Orders. (Part II of Wills and Deeds E, 1666 - 1675)
               130 fo.

1724 - 1734   Orders. (Bound with Wills, etc., 1723 - 1733) 212 pp.

Note: Abstracts of Lower Norfolk County Records, 1636-1646, were
published in the Virginia Magazine, Vol. 39, page 1 plus (1931).
    These abstracts were taken many years ago by Mr. Wilson Miles
Cary of Baltimore. We understand a number of early entries were
omitted. They were published under the name of Mrs. Rebecca Johnston
of the Virginia Historical Society. However she told me she merely
edited Mr. Cary's notes for publication and did not attempt to
compare them with the originals. Those checked back were found to
be correct in detail, but no effort has been made to fill in the
omissions. Perhaps that can be done later by some patient student.
                                                        B.F.

Lower Norfolk County Records
Wills and Deeds—C.
15th December 1651 – plus.

page 1.   Recorded 15 Jan. 1651/2. Dated 7 Nov. 1648. Agreement betw
Alice Mason, widow and relict of Mr. Francis Mason, dec'd and Mr.
Lemuell Mason of the one part and Mr. James Thelaball of the other part.
(1)   "That the said Lemuel Mason shall uppon demand give and assure
unto the said Mr Thelaball the Lands called the Mayne right against Hogg
Iland beinge about Two hundred acres, which the one halfe of the said
Hogg Iland, which Hogg Iland is to be devided by fower men to be in-
differently chosen, or by the said Lemuell and James, one of them to
make the devision, and thether to choose as they shall best agree"
(2)   Alice and Lemuell to give James "two thousand foote of sawen
planke".
(3)   Alice and Lemuell to give James "as much glasse and leade, as to
make fower such glasse windowes as are in the now dwelling house wherein
they remayne".
(4)   "That the said Alice and Lemuell shall uppon demand give and
Deliver unto the said James Six silver spoones"

Wit: Signed   Alice Mason
Tho: Lambert   Lemuell Mason
Rich: Conquest   James Thelaball
John Sibsey
Math: Phillippes

page 1. Recorded 7 Jan. 1651/2.   "Mary White aged 17: yeres or
thereabouts" sworn as a witness to the will of Capt: Leift: john
Gilham says he bequeathed all his estate in this country "unto his
brother in Lawe Mr Roger Fountayne" and appointed him his sole exor,
"onely did bequeath unto his Eldest sonne John Gilham his Rapier,
and his usuall worne seale gould Ringe And this is the full some of
his testament".   Signed   Marie x White
Sworn in Court 15 Jan 1651 (1651/2) by me Willm Jermy Clericus Cuy.

page 1. Recorded 7 Jan. 1651/2. Dated 24 Dec 1651. John Lownes
agrees to keep certain stock belonging to Capt Mathew Woods with the
increase until his return from Barbadoes.
Wit: Signed   John Lownes
Thos Goodrich
Geo Gosden
-
John Lownes, merchant, living in Elizabeth River in the County of Lower
Norfolk, sells Capt. Mathewe Wood, marriner, now in Virginia, for 2000

lbs of tobacco, certain cattle as above. This entry signed and
witnessed as above. Dates the same.

p.1. Account of charges laid out by Nathaniell Hayes at the funeral of
John Kennar. Totals 1163 lb tobo.

p.2. Will of Robt Powys of Linhaven in Virginia, Clarke.
Dated 2 December 1651. Prob. 12 Dec. 1651.
To daughter Mary Powys in England 16 head of cattle to be chosen out
     of whole stock, to be delivered in 3 years after day of decease
     in case she be then living "and shall or Doe arive in virginia
     within the tearme Aforesayd". Should she die the cattle to son
     Robert Powys.
To "my Loveing kinsman John Rich" 1 hhd tobo and 3 bbl corn to be
     delivered within one month of decease at the house of "Corronell
     Yardly".
To Katherine, the wife of James Phillips for token of love and "heir
     great payns and Care in tending and looking to me in the time of
     my scknesse" a 2 yr old heifer.
Residue of estate to son Robert, he exor.
Appoints "my Loveing frend Corronell Francis Yardley" and "Serjant Major
     Edward Windham" supervisors.
Wit: Signed   Robt Powes
E: Windham sec   Clerk
Johis Gilham
Adami A Bellamy

p.3. Bill of Sale. Recorded 15 Jan 1651/2. Edwd Cooper sells Andrew
Warner of Lynhaven, planter, for 1500 lb tobo, a parcel of land.
Dated 9th Nov 1647.   Signed   Edward x Cooper
Record states this was also recorded 12 Aug 1647 in the County Records.

p.3.   A Court held 10th April 1652.
                    Capt John Sibsey
                    Mr Cornelius Loyd
                    Mr Thomas Lambert
                    Mr Lemuell Mason   Commissioners.

p.3.   On petition of Savill Gaskin an attachmt granted him agst the
estate of W m Cleaver "he having Departed this County" for 331 lb tobo.

p.3. Attachmt to George Johnson agst est of Wm Cleaver for as much as
Johnson makes it appear as due

p.3. On petition of Lewes Fawell (Farwell) attachmt agst estate of
Wm Cleaver as he makes appear due.

p.3.   A Court 15th April 1652.
                Mr Cornelius Loyd
                Mr Thomas Lambert
                Capt Edward Windham
                Mr John Sidney
                Mr Lemuell Mason   Commissioners

p.3.   On petition of John Piggott, merchant, he to be pd amount due
from estate of Robert Eyre, gent., deceased.

p.3.   Symond Handcocke, attorney of Robte Cramphorne, makes it appear
there is due from the est of Robte Eyre dec'd "thurty pounds money
starl". It being a debt due for tobo rec'd by sd Eyer (sic) in his
lifetime of Ellis Browne for use of sd Cramphorne.

p.4.   Thos Watkins, atty of Will: Brooke, marriner, makes it appear
that Robte Eyre rec'd for Brooke 492 lb tobo in his lifetime. He to
be paid.

p.4.   Francis Emperor, Atty of Ellis Browne, makes it appear that Robte
Eyer dec'd owed Browne 647 lb tobo. He to be paid.

p.4.   John Custis "who intermarried with the relict and Administratrix
of Robt Eyer Deceased" and Simon Overzee Merchant hereby engage themselves in open Court in the sum of 20000 lb tobo to satisfy orders agt
the estate of Eyer, amounting to 7510 lb tobo, etc., etc. Quietus est
to Custis.

p.4.   On petition of Mary XXXXX Savill letters of admr granted her on
est of John Cooke dec'd, she having proved by oath that Cooke gave her
his estate.   (This name is Mary Savill)

p.4.   On petition of Mary Savill, order that Leftenant Collonell
Sidney, Mr Thos Bridg, Mr James Thelaball and Simon Landcoke be appointed to appraise the estate of John Cooke.

p.4.   Attachmt to Simond Overzee, merchant, against the estate of Wm.

Lewes for 4300 lb tobo "the sayd Lewes livinge out of the Country"

p.4.   Attachmt to Simond Overzee, merchant, agst est of Wm Janes, decd.,
for 1725 lb tobo due by bill.

p.4.   Attachmt to Simond Overzee, merchant, for 2 hhd tobo containing
504 lb tobo, of Wm Lucas "lying in the house of Thomas Hall".

p.4.   Mary Savill admrx of John Cooke decd ordered to pay debt of 1729
lb tobo to Simond Overzee from the estate.

p.4.   Attachmt to Simond Overzee agst est of Capt Samson Lane for
L 80. money sterling for 4 guns.

p.4.   Roger Fountayne ordered to pay Simond Overzee debt of 2120 lb tobo

p.5.   Order that Roger Fountayne, admr of John Gilham dec'd, be paid
5865 lb tobo due from the estate.

p.5.   Cause depending betw Robaart Darby and Rouland Morgan referred
to next Court.

p.5.   Roger Fountayne, admr of John Gilham dec'd, ordered to pay
Laurence Plummer debt of 500 lb tobo made by Gilham in his lifetime.

p.5.   Roger Fountayne, admr of John Gilham, ord to pay Lemuell Mason,
gent., debt of 330 lb tobo.
Also: ordered to pay Richd Lipscombe debt of 7000 lb tobo.
Also: ordered to pay Henry Brakes debt of 2000 lb tobo for several
        bills.

p.5.   Letters of admr to Elizabeth Causon, widow, on estate of Thomas
Causon dec'd, her late husband.

p.5.   Judgt ack by George Johnson to John Dyer for paymt of 430 lb tobo.

p.5.   Attachmt granted the last Court to Geo Johnson agst est of Wm.
Cleaver "the said Cleaver beinge out of this County". Judgt now for
604 lb tobo.

1652

p.5   Judgt to Savill Gaskin agst est of Wm Cleaver for 331 lb tobo.

p.5   Judgt to John Rice, Atty of Richd Clerke, Wine Cooper, agst est
of Roger Fletcher dec'd for L 73. 7. 0 Sterling "due upon bond for
goods transported into this Collony".

p.5   Tho Bridge gent ordered to deliver up all bills, bonds, etc., in
the estate of Roger Fletcher decd to James Rice, atty of Richd Clarke
within 10 days.

p.5   Attachmt to X'pofer Burrowes gent agst est of George Migh for 613
lb tobo.

p.5   Attachmt to Robt Powes agst est of George Migh for 350 lb tobo.

p.5   Judgt to Tho Bridge agst est of Jno Claus decd for 144 lb tobo.

p.6   Thos Daynes, atty of Geo Migh, was arrested at suit of Lemuell
Mason, gent., exor of will of Francis Mason, gent., dec'd., and fails
in coming to Court. No security taken. The Sheriff ordered to produce
him at next Court.

p.6   Tho Daynes, as atty for George Migh, arrested at suit of James
Thelaball and no security taken. The Sheriff to bring him to next Court.

p.6   On petition of Coll Francis Yardley, attachmt to him agst est of
Robt Atkinson, merchant, for L 200. Sterling.

p.6   On petition of James Starlinge, attachmt to him agst est of Wm
Cleaver for 1044 lb tobo due by bill.

p.6   John Carraway who married the relict of Roger Williams, dec'd,
ordered to take into his custody all cattle belonging to the orphans
of said Williams until next Orphan's Court.

p.6   In cause betw John Holmes and Roger Fountayne admr of Jno Gilham
dec'd concerning one Addam Bellamy upon full hearing, order that
Bellamy serve out his time with Holmes, etc., etc. Some detail of
terms following.

1652

p.6   Tho. Lambert, gent, makes it appear there is due him from John
Dyer, by bill, 1159 lb tobo. Dyer ordered to pay.

p.6   Cause betw Edward Hall, Chirur', and Wm Robinson to be determined
at next Court by request of Robinson.

p.6   That Henry Westgate made it appear at Court held Dec 1650 an
order was granted him agst James Smith for payment of 700 lb tobo. That
Smith pd the debt but refuses to pay Court charges, etc.

p.6   John Laine arrested at suit of Wm Robinson fails to appear. Order
that the Sheriff produce him at next Court.

p.6   A servant of George Migh killed a heifer at Linhaven. The owner
not fully known. Order that Migh restore another heifer within one year
"And to be disposed of by the Commissioners of this County for the
benefitt of the poore children in Line Haven parish aforesaid".

p.6   On petition of Francis Laud (or Land ?) that there is due him
1150 lb tobo from George Hawkins, order for payment.

p.6   That Francis Laud (or Land ?) has arrested Tho Hall to this
Court and no cause for action. Order that he pay Hall 40 lb tobo.

p.6   Cause of James Sterlinge pltf and Geo Hawkins deft to next Court,
also Hawkins pltf and Sterling deft to next Court.

p.6   That Edward Gradwell decd made his will and that his estate is of
no great value. Order that Henery Brakes to whom he left most of his
est take all into his custody, paying the debts.

p.7   In cause betw Thomas Ivey pltf and Henery Merritt deft, order that
Merritt "returne to the house of the said Ivey and there to use his best
industry for the finishinge upp of one kill of Earthen Ware: the said
Ivey assisting him with two men according to a condi'con made betweene
them, And the said Ivey to gett the Kill finished upp fitting to burne
the aforesaid Earthen Weare And further the said Ivey is to bringe in
a full and just account of all disbursments and receipts whatsoever laid
out or received by the said Ivey since their partnershipp at the next
Court". If the work not performed Ivey to deliver to Merritt "his bedd

and workinge Tooles with Corne to keepe him till the next Court and then
to be heard and determined".

Note: As one drives through this part of Virginia, in the sandy soil
there appear great streaks of sticky red clay and other great streaks of
a blueish gray something we used to know as fullers earth. If there are
brick kilns or potteries around Norfolk I never happen to have seen
them, though it is to be presumed they are there. In the old days this
fullers earth was used to make drain pipes, to make paint, to pack
horses' feet to protect them, etc.
        The origin of the North Carolina potters to the south has never
been settled. Not that they care a hoot where they came from. They are
there, that is all. At Jugtown (a name that delights me) near Southern
Pines and Pinehurst (on side roads dusty in summer and muddy in winter)
the tradition is that these potters escaped, in the early days, from
Jamestown. But from the foregoing entry it may have been from the
Norfolk area. They always were a quarrelsome lot, inclined to be quite
fond of the jug or jar or whatever they kept it in - and still keep it
in. However their pottery is just fine. So good it seems impossible for
us to get out of North Carolina without at least one more piece in our
baggage. Five dollars will provide Christmas gifts for all your superior
friends.   B.F.

p.7   That Coll Francis Yardley be nonsuited, having caused Rowland
Morgan to be arrested and not appearing himself or anyone for him.

p.7   On petition of Anne Rutherford, an orphan, order that Thos Hall
her Brother in Law be her Guardian, and likewise Francis Laud (or Land)
deliver the cattle belonging to her according to the a/c given the
Court by Hall.

p.7   On petition of Thos Hall who intermarried with Margery Rutherford
one of the orphans of - - Rutherford (the first name left blank in the
record), that Francis Laud (or Land ?) who intermarried with the
relict of the said Rutherford, deliver the cattle, etc., etc.

Note: This name Laud or Land is a devil to read. In one entry it is
certainly Laud. In the next entry it will just as certainly be Land.
And there you are - nowhere.   B.F.

p.7   Capt John Sibsey, attorney of Arthur Browne, makes it appear that
there is due from George Migh 126 lb tobo. The Sheriff having arrested
Thomas Daynes, attorney of Migh, and no security taken and he not appearing, order that the Sheriff produce Daynes or pay the debt.

p.7   At the last Court an attachmt was granted Lewes Farwall agst the estate of Wm Cleaver for 239 lb tobo. Judgmt for this.

p.7   Simon Overzee has due to him from Wm Robinson, cooper, a sum of
tobacco. Paymt ordered.

p.7   Tho Bushrode arrested Capt Edw. Windham to this Court and does not
appear to prosecute. He is nonsuited.

p.7   Tho Bushrode arrested Lemuell Mason, gent., attorney of Tho: Lee,
to this Court and not appearing to prosecute is nonsuited.

p.7   According to instructions from the Council, William Daynes, gent.,
is appointed "High Shereive for this County of Lower Norfolk".

p.7   Constables chosen by this Court:

1:   William Robinson for the Eastearne branch in Elizabeth River
2:   Thomas Herne (or Horne ?) for the Southerne branch i'bm:
3:   Richard Sternell for the Westerne branch i'bm:
4:   Trusteram Mason from Daniell Tanners Creeke to Capt Willoughbyes
5:   Robte Fowler for the Little Creeke in Lynhaven parish
6:   Simond Cornix for the Westearne shoare ibm:
7:   John Dyer for the Easterne Shoare ibm:

p.7   Finis huius Curiae:
               per me Willm Jermy   Clearicus Cuy'.

p.8   "15th of Aprill Ao D'm 1652:
       Ordered to be Recorded"

p.8   That Rowland Morgan owes Jno Holmes 170 lb tobo. Order that paymt
be made in 10 days. Dated 6 March 1651/2. Signed Lemuell Mason.

p.8   Recorded 15 April 1652. "Thomas Tooker, aged 38 years or thereabouts", sworn saith that the year he lived with Mr. Lambert he went
aboard Simon Overzee's ship together with Mr Lambert, who took with him
his man, John Baptist. That Baptist refused to go ashore again with his
said master, "sayenge that he would goe upp to the Governor for he

would serve but fower yeres". But Overzee told Lambert to take Baptist
"for he had soūld the said Baptist unto him for his life tyme, and he
should serve his life tyme", etc.
Dated 15 April 1652.   Signed   Tho Tooker

Note: What kind of slavery was this ? Criminal, religious, political,
the bullying of the upper classes, or what ?   B.F.

page 8.   Will of Edward Gradwell of the Little Creek in the parish of
Lynhaven, planter, "beinge sicke of boddy".
Dated 3rd Dec 1651. Prob 15 April 1652.
To Henery Brakes of the same parish all goods, cattle, household stuff,
etc.
That John Cubbish "have house and ground for himselfe and another duer-
      inge the tearme of the lease".
To John Stronge, servant to Henery Brakes, a 2 yr old heifer at the
      expiration of his time.
To Maudlinge Kempe, dau of Mary Kemp, widow, a cow.
Wit: Signed   the marke of
Henery Westgate   Edward: E: Gradwell
John Spencer
Nicholas x Mason

p.8   Inventory of est of Edw: Gradwell given 15 April 1652 by Henery
Brakes. Cattle and a small amount of household goods.

p.8   Inv of estate of Capt John Gilham, decd, of Lynhaven in Co. of
Lower Norfolk, 12 March 1651/2.
Includes "for 8: ould bookes"   0100
Totals 4214 lb tobo.
Assets include debts due for tobacco:
Capt: Sibsey   0300
Mr: Tho: Goodrich   0250
John Taylor   4000
Simond Barrowe   0050
Henery Porter   0083
Bill of Wm Singleton's assigned by Richard Lipscombe   0850
from Ensigne Sterlinge   0016

The totall some of the Estate is 12976 (lb tobo.)
                          Signed   Francis Laud   (or Land)
                                   Simond Barrowe
                                   John Taylor   Appraisors

p.9   Presented in Court 15th April 1652 by John Custis, who married
the Admrx of Robte Eyre dec'd, and Simond Overzee mercht, and ordered
to be recorded.

	lb tobo
Imprimis to Simond Hancocke by order for a man servant	1500
To Wm Robinson by order	0794
to him by an other order	1150
more to Simond Hancocke by order	0485
to mr Moseley by order	1100
to mr Cornelius Loyd by order	0504
to Lewes Farmall by order	0262
more to him	0431
to Laurence Phillipps by order	0256
to Mrs Yates wid' by order 3: barrells of Corne	0450
more to her in tob:	0040
mr Cornelius Loyd more by order	0240
to mr Daynes	0300
	- - - -
	7510

Bills tendered by them in Court and not received
vizt

Mr Brice his bill	0450
Edward Standley	0252
mr John Piggotte	0136
Tho: Cartwrights	0164
mr Sprys	2000
Simon Handcocke	0180
John Sidney gent:	0502
more to this Estate due one heifer appraised at	0400
	- - - -
	4084

Mr Eyres Estate appraised at 14500 lb tobo
Ballence   03006
Totall   11594

page 9
Lower Norfolk   Ordered to be recorded this 15th day of Aprill 1652
                Depositions of Stephen Key, George Wright and Richard
                Founder. Ages not shown in record.
"Whereas John Cooke lately deceased that uppon his death bedd hath made
his will unto Mary Savill before the said three abovenamed witnesses.
Stephen Key demanded of him if he would make noe will, for the disposinge
of his Estate he onely answered that the longest liver take all, thafore
said Key askinge him againe if Mary Savill should not enjoy it, he
answered him againe YES who should Else. The next day after the said
Key desired him to make his will to her or else his mother, or his

brother would come and Enjoy it, he answered how should they come the
said Key said by the Shipping, aye but they shall never have it, if I
live, and more saith not".

                              Signed   Stephen Key
                                         George x Wright
                                         Rich: x Founder

Jurat in Cur: die and anno sup'ris.

p.9   Recorded 15 April 1652.
         "The deposition of Peeter Barnester Gunner of the Shipp
          Virginia mercht belonginge to mr Simond Overzee" (His
          age not shown on record)
"Bringeth tydings that the said Shipp being cast away in the River of
Piscataway in Newe England, the gunnes whereof were landed on the said
Shoare which Gunnes were deminished by One Capt: Samson Lane, he takinge
fower of them with him to the Barbadoes, and further saith not:"
                              Signed   Peter Barnester
Sworn 15 April 1652.

p.9   At a Speciall Court held the 22th day of Aprill Anno Dm: 1652
         at the instance of Richard Richardson
Present
         Capt John Sibsey   Mr John Sidney
         mr Cornelius Loyd   Mr Wm Moseley   Commissioners

p.9   Judgt to Rd Richardson mercht agst Jno Lownes for 1990 lb beef
and 245 lb tobo.

p.10   A Court held 1st June 1652.
Present
         Collo Francis Yardley   Mr Lemuell Mason
         Leift: Coll: Cornelius Loyd Mr Xpofer Burrowes
         Major Thomas Lambert   Mr Francis Emperor
         Mr John Sidney   Mr Thomas Bridge
         Mr William Moseley   Mr Thomas Goodrich
                                        Jurant' Comissrs

p.10   At the last Grand Assembly power being given to the Commissioners
of each County for selecting Clerks in their several places, Wm Jermy
is herewith appointed Clerk of the Court of Lower Norfolk.

p.10   William Daynes gent sworn High Sheriff. Thomas Tooker sworn Under
Sheriff. Mr. Cornelius Loyd security for Daynes.

p.10   Francis Emperor having entered several actions agst Geo Heigham
and the Sheriff returning "a non est inventus" (does not have anything)
attachmt agst Heigham's estate.

p.10   Divers suits agst Thos Daynes, gent., as attorney of George Migh,
who is out of this colony. Daynes promises not to transport any of the
property out of the colony, Lemuell Mason to take choice of certain bills
to pay himself from Migh's estate.

p.10   Cause betw Tho Sayer pltf and Francis Emperor gent deft referred
to next Court.

p.10   Richd Conquest gent admr of John Kempe dec'd ordered to submit
an account of the estate.

p.10   That Francis Laud (or Land ?) "beinge gone for England", his
attorney, Robt Powes, ordered to pay debt of 346 lb tobo due to Simond
Overzee.

p.10   John Martin ordered to deliver to Simond Overzee "Three peeces of
Linnen Cloath, alsoe Twelve silver spoones" which he "detyneth from him"

p.10   John Piggett gent to be pd debt of 4732 lb tobo from estate of
Robert Eyre.

p.10   On petition of Henery Woodhouse, gent., attorney of Jno Mendham
who married the sister of Tho Leech decd, administration of the estate
to Mendham.

p.10   Cause betw Capt John Sibsey pltf and Thos Daynes attorney of Geo
Migh referred to next Court.

p.11   Mary Savill admrx of John Cooke ordered to pay debt of 528 lb
tobo due Thos Alexander mercht.

p11.   James Starlinge ordered to pay 899 lb tobo of next crop to Geo
Hawkins in settlement of suit.

p.11   In cause betw Tho. Hall guardian of Anne Rutherford an orphan, and Francis Laud (or Land ?) the cattle to be divided by Mr: Henery Woodhouse and Mr. Xpofer Burrowes.

p.11   Cause betw Jno Lownes pltf and Wm Moseley gent deft referred to next Court.

p.11   John Lownes ordered to pay Richd Chapman debt of 426 lb tobo.

p.11   That John Rice chirurgeon arrested Wm Robinson and did not appear against him. Is nonsuited.

p.11   Attachmt to Jno Williams agst the estate of Tho Woodward, surveyor, in hands of Col Francis Yardley for 1000 lb tobo "the said Woodward beinge out of this Country".

p.11   Cause betw John Carraway pltf and Richd Woster to next Court.

p.11   Judgt confessed by Major Thos Lambert gent, attorney of Richard Trevor, for 624 lb tobo, for paymt to Thos Dadford attorney of Timothy Ives.

p.11   Cause betw Coll Francis Yardley and Jno Lownes to next Court.

p.11   Attachmt to Major Tho Lambert gent agst estate of Richd Trevor for 5000 lb tobo.

p.11   Case betw Thos Ivey pltf and Henery Merritt deft fully settled. Merritt to pay Ivey 1928 lb tobo on a/c. "and that the Kell of Earthen Ware now to be burned together with all mat'ialls belonginge whatsoever about the makinge and finishinge of former Earthen ware be Equally divided betweens the said Ivey and the said Merritt". Ivey to deliver to Merritt his tools, bedding, etc.

p.11   The Commissioners to pay Laurence Phillipps 15 lb tobo for every meal they take in time of Court.

p.11   Certificate for 200 acres to Simond Hancocke for transporting Randall Hewett, John Cooper, Simon Robinson and George Gay.

1652

p.11   Certificate for 200 acres to Simond Hancocke for transporting
James Onthery (may be also read as Outkcry), George Hudson, Peter
Weldinge and Richard Bitoge.
Note: The names Onthery and Bitoge are of course in error. The name
Weldinge may be a form of the Virginia name Weldon.
      Simond Hancocke's widow, Sarah Handcocke, patented land in Lower
Norfolk in 1657.   B.F.

p.12.   Constables to give notice to all men in their limits to have
their arms fixed to be ready suddenly for the Indians. And further that
William Johnson, smith, fix any man's arms brought to him and be paid
from the levy.

p.12   The following ordered to bring in their lists of tytheables to
the Clerk of the Court by 15th July.

For the Easterne Shoare in Lynhaven   Voll: Lovell
for the Westerne Shoar there   Robte Powes
for the Little Creeke   Tho: Ward
for the Easterne branch in Elizabeth River   Richard Foster
for the Southerne branch there   Lewes Farmall
for the Westerne branch there   Francis Fleetwood
from Daniell Tanners Creeke to Apt Willoughbyes Thomas Ivey
                              Signed
                                    Willm Jermy

p.12   Recorded 1 June 1652.
          Att a Quarter Court held at James Citty the 6th of November 1651:
                 Sir William Berkeley, Governor
          Present
                 Sir Tho: Luntsford   L. generall
                 Coll: Sam: Mathewes
                 Col: Wm: Barnard
                 Coll: Tho: Pettus
                 Coll: George Ludlowe
                 Adjutant Freeman
                 Coll: Hill
                 Coll Rich: Lee
                 Major Wm. Taylor

p.12   Richard Conquest ordered to pay debt 1130 lb tobo to Leif: Coll:
Walter Chiles with 2 years interest.
                              Test   John Jennings
p.12   Receipt, dated 8 Nov 1651. To Richard Conquest for 1130 lb tobo.
Wit: Signed   Walter Chiles
Wm Edwards.

p.12   P of A. 7 Sept 1651. Recorded 1st June 1652. Francis Wells of
the parish of St Giles in the fields in the County of Middlesex, Gent.,
(England), to "my trusty and well beloved frend John Pigot of Virginia
Merchant and Citizen and merchant taylor of London", to receive debts
and goods from persons now resident in Virginia.
Wit: Signed   Francis Wells
Richard Tanner   x
Roger Conyers   his marke
William Jenkins

p.13   Deed of Gift. 17 April 1652. Symon Hancock gives his God-son
John Williams a cow calf in this manner: the first calf it brings for
use of sd Jno Williams, the third calf to be for use of Elizabeth
Carraway. If Jno Williams die before 21 the cattle to Eliz Carraway.
If she die before coming of age the cattle "to John Carraway his second
or third Childe and for the better looking after these Cattle it is my
desire that the father or Mother shall have the male increase, and this
to bee Recorded as a free gifte".
Wit: Signed   the marke of
William Moseley   x
John Pigott   Symon Hancock

p.13   Deed. 8 August 1643. Edward Windham of Linhaven in the Lower
County of Nowe Norfk in Virginia, gent., sells James Starling of Lin-
haven, planter, for 900 lb tobo, as by his specialty dated the 1st of
July last past, 250 acres on westermost branch of Samuel Bennetts
Creek, Easterly and bounded Southerly on land of William East and North-
erly on "land of Capt Adam Thoroogood which is now in the occupation
of Henry Hill", and Westerly into the woods. This 250 acres being half
of 500 acres patented in the name of John Lanckfeild 10 Feb 1637/8.
Wit: Signed   Edward Windham
Robt Tyas

p.13   Patent. 28 July 1648. Sir Wm Berkeley, kt., Governor, etc., to
Capt Francis Yardley, 590 acres in Co. of Lower Norfolk, on a Creek
called Samuell Bennetts Creek, betw land granted Jno Lankfeild now
belonging to Thomas Davis and Addam Thurrowgoode and Timber Necke being
taken up by Capt Francis Yardley. Also bounds on Needhams Marsh.
Considerable technical description of boundries omitted here. This Land
for transporting 12 persons into the Colony, their names not shown in
this record book.   Signed   William Berkeley

Endorsement: Francis Yardley of Lynhaven in the Co of Lower Norfolk,
gent., assigns the above land to Christopher Burrowes of the same place,
gent., for a term of years (9 yrs). Dated 10 Nov 1649.
Wit: Signed   Fran: Yardley
Edw: Standley
Jacobi x Topham

p.14   Ordered to be recorded 15 June 1652.
Governor's order dated 20 May 1652 to settle dif betw Richd Richardson
mercht, pltf., and John Lownes, deft. That Lownes deliver the 3 saws in
question to Richardson and be pd 400 lb tobo by him.
"per me Willm Jeimy" (sic)   Signed   Cornelius Loyd

p.14   "Ordered to be Recorded this 15th of June 1652"
"Lower Norfolk   In the matters of difference depending betweene John
Lownes and Richard Richardson mercht, It beinge by them referred to us
for the Ordering and Endinge thereof: Upon the full hearinge of all
differences betweene them it is by us Ordered that the said Lownes make
paym't of the seme of Three hundred forty and two pounds of tob: and
caske unto the said Richardson or his assigns If in case Laurence
Phillipps make not payment thereof to the said Richardson within 14:
dayes als Execucon. It alsoe (is) further ordered that the said Richardson aske Mrs Lownes forgivenes presently before us for abusinge her by
scandalous and abusive termes likewise we doe order and fine the said
Lownes and the said Richardson One hundred and fifty pounds of tobacco a
peice for useinge of Unlawfull Weapons in a most rioutous manner uppon
the Sabboth day to be paid for the use of the County And further that
the said Lownes and Richardson give to each other a generall discharge".
                                Signed   Cornelius Loyd
                                          Thos Lambert
                                          Francis Emperor

p.15   Deed. "last day of January 1643. (1643/4). Robert Hayes of
Little Creek in the par of Lynhaven in the Co of Lower Norfolk, sells
Wm Burrough of same par, 200 acres. This being part of 700 acres granted
to Henery Southerne on E side of Lynhaven River, which patent was again
renewed by Capt Richd Popeley and taken in his name and since sold to
sd Hayes. The land to begin on a Creek running E out of Lynhaven River
at the place "where the Indian path lyeth over it and from that place
where the Indian bridge did lye over the said Creeke", etc.
Wit: Robte Dunster   Signed   Robte Hayos
      Thos Hayes
      William Lucas

Endorsed: That Wm Burrough, by letter of atty, dated 23 Jan 1641/2,
gave to Christopher Burrough power to transact business for his estate.
That by several letters of release dated 5 Sept 1642, and another dated
22 Oct 1642, the sd Wm desired the sale of his plantation, the above 200
acres. This land now assigned, for 1800 lb tobo, to Cesar Puggett (I
cannot make this name into anything but Puggett. It is not Suggett. B.F.)
Dated 2 Feb 1643/4.   Signed   Xpofer Burrough
Wit: Tho Tooker
      Will: Lucas

Also Endorsed: That Wm Lucas of Lynhaven assigns Thomas Hall and

John Dyer the above bill of sale and the land, 200 acres. Dated 10 Feby
1651/2.
Wit: William Bence   Signed   Wm Lucas
      Andrewe Warner

p.16   At a Court held the 16th August 1652.
Present   Coll Francis Yardley   Mr Lemuell Mason
          Left: Coll: Cornelius Loyd Mr Xpofer Burrowes
          Major Thomas Lambert   Mr Francis Emperor
          Mr John Sidney   Mr Thomas Bridge
          Mr William Moseley   Mr Tho: Goodrich
                                              Commissioners

p.16.   In dif betw Richd Scanes vs Richd Chapman no cause for action.

p.16   In dif betw Nathaniell Carter pltf vs Jas Simmons deft, Simmons
to pay Carter 300 lb tobo.

p.16. Attachmt to Andrew Nicholls agst est of Tho Marsh for 560 lb tobo,
sd Marsh being out of the Colony.

p.16   Wm Moseley, gent, to pay Jno Lownes 100 lb tobo due by bill.

p.16   Probate of will of Capt John Sibsey to Elizabeth Sibsey, widow,
she being sole extrx.

p.16   On petition of Eliz Sibsey, widow, the following appointed to
appraise the est of her dec'd husband: Lemuel Mason, Jno Hill gent,
Tho Ivey and Geo Kempe.

p.16   Geo Migh ordered to pay 454 lb tobo due by bill to Eliz Sibsey,
widow, extrx of Jno Sibsey. Migh being out of the Colony to pay interest.

p.16   Dif betw Edwd Hall, chirurgeon and Col Francis Yardley to next
Court.

p.16   Dif betw Thos Bridge gent pltf and Richd Conquest deft, appealed
by Conquest to Genl Court 6th Oct next at James Citty. Mr Lemuell Mason
goes his security.

p.16   In dif betw Leift Coll Cornelius Loyd in behalf of that County
and Richd Conquest gent, Conquest appeals to the Genl Court held 6th
Oct next at James Cityy. Mr Lemuell Mason goes his security.

p.16   "In cause of complaint b't Jane Latham and John Cubbidge def't
It is ordered that the said Jane Latham returne home to her masters
house And there to dee her service as she ought to doe, And that the
said Cubbidge forbeare strikinge her untill the next Court. And uppon
her misdemeanor to be carried to the next Justice of peace and there to
receive condigne punishm't".

Note: God in his Mercy was supposed to protect the poor working girl.
Alas ! He did not always do that. This one evidently flared back at
her master and he had to hit her. I too have had them I'd liked to have
hit. And, shame upon me, I did kick one once. Not that she did not
deserve it – that sanctimonius bitch that tried to seduce my friend the
Methodist minister in my pantry. As usual I was to blame. Me, a good High
Church Episcopalian, ever letting a Methodist minister in my house. It
might be that said Cubbidge was right in not strikeinge her until after
the next Court. I might remark that the Methodist was a right handsome
young man at that !   B.F.
Note No.2: Condigne – deserved, merited, suitable.   B.F.

p.16   Coll Francis Yardley and Leift: Coll: Cornelius Loyd in open
Court, on behalf of Mr. Wm Moseley, engage themselves to save harmless
Elizabeth Sibsey, widow, extrx of Capt Jno Sibsey deod, from a debt due
by Bill of Exch under the hand of sd Moseley due to Capt Sibsey, and
assigned by him to Edward Maior (Major) in his lifetime.

Note: This name Major, a surname, used frequently later as a first
name in the old families, is disconcerting to say the least.   B.F.

p.16   Dif betw Rd Conquest pltf and Robt Powes deft to next Court.
(This kind of entry means nothing, takes up space, but we have to have
it to make the record complete. B.F.)

p.16   Dif betw Jno Lownes and Coll Francis Yardley to next Court.
Yardley ordered to bring in Wm Eale a bricklayer, late servant to Jno
Lownes, as a witness.

p.17   John Sidney gent acks sale of 2 dividends of land in the head of
the Easterne branch of Elizabeth River in the County of Lower Norfolk,
called by names of Black Walnutt Tree necke and Harryes Necke to George
Kemp.

p.17   Dif betw Thos Ivey; pltf, and Rd Conquest gent, deft; concerning
a tract of land. Conquest appeals to the Genl. Court. Lemuell Mason goes
his bond.

p.17   Certificate for 150 acres to Isacke Morgan for transporting
himself, Mary Showell and Anne Littleton into this colony.

p.17   Col Fr: Yardley to pay Jno Lownes 1200 lb tobo due by bill.

p.17   Admr of est of Edw: Butler dec'd to Major Thos Lambert.

p.17   Coll Fr. Yardley having obtained attachmt agst est of Robert
Attkinson, now craveth judgt, which he is to have unless Attkinson
appears at next Court.

p.17   Probate of will of Peter Barrnes granted to Richd Eastwood, he
being sole exor named in the will.
(This name shown here as Barrnes appears several times and still I am
uncertain as to what it actually was.   B.F.)

p.17   An Orphans Court to be held 15th Sept next at the house of
Lawrence Phillipps, and also then and there a Court "for the setting
of the Malitia" and for appointing Surveyors of the High Wayes.

p.17   Finis of this Court. Signed William Jejmy (sic). - Jermy.

p.17   Will of John Sibsey of Elizabeth River in the County of Lower
Norfolk, gent.
Dated 15 July 1652. Ordered to be Recorded 16 Aug 1652.
Land called Craney Point, now in the possession of Robert Woody to be
     sold for payment of debts "suddenly after my decease".
To wife Elizabeth Sibsey all plate and servants.
To dau Mary Sibsey residue of land adj Craney Point.
To Henery Wake land now in possession of Richd Pinner after expiration
     of lease now made.
To wife residue of lands.
To Margery Wickstead, widdow, 500 lb tobo. To her dau Elizabeth a cow
     and a yewe.
Residue of goods and chattels to be div in 3 parts, 2 parts to wife and
     the 3rd part to dau: "And if it shall happen my said daughter depte
     this life before Mr Conquest her husband without issue" that one

Half of her est return to wife and one half to go "to Mr Richard
Conquest my said Daughters husband"
To "my beloved Brother in Lawe Thomas Lambert One Pistle and my feather".
To William Jermy (the Clerk) "my blacke hilted Rapier and belt" and
debts due from him.
To daughter 6 silver spoons and one servant "either my servant John
Paine, or David Southerly which my said daughter will".
Wife sole extrx. Supervisors friends Tho Lambert and William Jermy.
Wit: Tho: Ivey   Signed   John Sibsey
       Trus Mason

p.18   Recorded 16 August 1652.
By Court order, 1 June 1652, all differences betw Thomas Hall on behalf
of the children of Richard Rudderford late in the tuition of Francis
Land, and the said Francis Land on behalf of himself, order that Robte
Powis, attorney of the sd Francis Land, pay to Tho Hall for the children,
before the last of Nov next, 700 lb tobo, in consideration of a steer
belonging to the children sold by Land. Further order that Powis give
to Hall for the sole use of Ann Rudderford, "one meete an Decent stoufe
sute of Clothes becoming the ranke and quality of her the said Ann
together with Change of headlinen hankerchiefs shifts neckclothes and
aprons with a payer of shooes and stockins answerable within twenty
dayes after the date hereof". Both payments to be made from est of sd
Francis Land. Dated 5 Aug 1652.
                                    Signed   Henry Woodhouse
                                              X'pfor Burrowes

p.18   Ordered Recorded 16 Aug 1652.
That (we) Collonell William Clawborne (sic) and Leftenant Colonell
Cornelius Loyd, arbitrators of a dif betw George Fletcher, gent, admr
of Capt: William Duglis and Cumpaney, and Mr John Straton now husband
of the wife of Thomas Causon dec'd, that Straton pay Fletcher 6000 lb
tobo owed by Causon. Dated 17 August 1652.
                                    Signed   William Clauborne
                                              Cornelius Loyd

Note: And yet there are still fools who quibble about the spelling of
the names of their ancestors. If the aristocratic Claibornes (they have
always been aristocratic) can stand this, then what about you obscure
ones ?   B.F.
Let me hasten to explain that I am not especially fond of every
Claiborne that I've ever seen (God forbid !), but there are those
that make up for all the rest - the beautiful Mrs. Guy for instance. B.F.

p.18   Will of Peter Barrns. Dated 17 July 1652. Recorded 16 Aug 1652.
"I make my loving mate Richard Eastwood my sole Executor".

(continued)

The will of Peter Barrns (continued)

To Elizabeth Windett dau of Edmond Windett a cow calf.
"I give unto Marry that is now servant to Mr Thos Wright" a calf to be
    delivered to her a week after she is free.
Wit: John Finch   Signed   Peter x Barrns

p.18   A suit long depending betw John Straton pltf and Mrs Sarah Gookin
deft on behalf of the orphans of Capt Adam Thorowgood. Now Stratton on
behalf of himself and Capt Edward Windham on behalf of Mrs Gookin and
the orphans agree concerning the land in question. Stratton to reling
all claim to 600 acres on Eastern Shore of Lynhaven River according to
a survey made by Edmund Scharbarrow. Also Stratton to relinq claim to a
parcel of land cleared and sold by Mr John Gookin to Mr Tho Cason being
about 20 acres.
       That Mrs Gookin shall from henceforth cease to molest him the sd
John Stratton concerning 200 acres granted to Robert Came and by him
bequeathed unto Ann Thorowgood the daughter of Capt Adam Thorowgood:
provided that sd Jno Stratton "doe suffer her to injoy the same peaceably"
etc., etc. This agreement dated 20 March 1645/6.
Wit: William Edwards   Signed   Edward Windham
       X'pfor Burrowes   John x Stratton

p.19   Inventory of est of Thomas Casson, dec'd.
Appraised 26 June 1652, by X'pfor Burrowes, Thos Hall, Robt Davis and
Edward Cannon. Totals 28170 lb tobo.
Includes: lb tobo
Item   two seasoned men servants, one for three years the
        other for fower yeares   4000
        one maide servant for one yeare and a halfe or there
        abouts   0600
        three new men and boy servants   4500

Note: This inventory is another evidence that persons coming to this
country might live, but more likely would not. The seasoned servants
therefore more valuable than the green (or new) ones.   B.F.

p.20   Ordered to be Recorded this 16th of August 1652.
"Edward Hall Churrgion came before us this 25th day of July and did take
his Corporall oath that he did goe in feare that Coll: Francis Yardley
will doe him some boddily harme, or burne his houses, and that he doth
not demand out of malice or for vexa'con, but very feare of some hurt
to be done to his boddy or houses, and therefore he Earnestly urged to
have a warr: for the peace to be granted against him the said Coll:
Francis Yardley, which we have promised to performe, for his security
by personall demanding the same, witnes our hands the day and yeare
above written"   Signed   X'pfer Burrough
                                               Tho: Bridge
                        (continued)

1652

The Yardley incident (continued).

According to our promise we went to Coll: Yardley and demanded suerty of the peace, and in respect of his place and for other reasons accepted of his promise in the word of a gentleman that he would keepe the same towards the said Hall:

Signed   X'pfer Burrough
Tho: Bridge

Note: It is quite evident here that Col. Yardley was not a gentleman in the first place. Quite sure in his own conceit that he was, he would have been much surprised to have known that at this late date we merely consider that he was a bully and an ass. To be sure not the first and far from the last that we have had to put up with in Virginia.   B.F.

p.20   At the Sessions held the 16th day of August Anno D'm 1652.
Present

Coll: William Clayborne Secret: Mr: Lemuel Mason
Coll: Francis Yardley   Mr: Xpfer Burrowh
Left: Coll: Cornelius Loyd   Mr: Francis Emperor
Major Thomas Lambert   Mr: Thomas Bridge
Leift: Coll: John Sidney   Mr: Thomas Goodrich
Mr: Wm Moseley   Commissioners

p.20   The Grand Jury
    Tho Sayer   Lancaster Lovett
    Robte Fowler   John Martin
    George Ashall   Edward Cannon
    Henery Snayle   John Dyer
    Gyles Collins   Richard Whitehurst
    Thomas Addams   Andrewe Nicholls
    John Lownes gent   X'pfer Rivers
                                                Jurant

p.20   Agnes Holmes, wife of John Holmes of the Little Creek in the Co of Lower Norfolk, planter, indicted for beating Useba Rider on 20th Oct, whereof he died.

p.20   Laurence Phillips of Elizabeth River in the Co of Lower Norfolk, planter, indicted for assaulting and killing Richard Joanes in 1651.

p.21   "The Grand Jury abovesaid uppon Evidence given in, as concerninge Lawrence Phillipps returned therein verdict Ignoramus And as concerning Agnes Holmes aforesaid they returned Billa vera".

1652

p.21   "The Jury of Life and Death"

Thomas Ivey	Richard Joanes
Henery Barlowe	Robte Bowers
Wm Wilson	Peter Rigleworth
Thomas Watkins	John Stratton
John Carraway	John Taylor
Thomas Greene	Henery Robinson

"This Jury of Life and Death concerninge Agnes Holmes standinge at the
Barr, and uppon full hearinge of the Evidence against her returned their
veredict Not Guilty: of the killinge of the aforesaid Useba Rider for
that which she stood Indicted aforesaid"

p.21   A Meeting of the Comm'rs for Ordering of the Malitia 15th Sept
       1652

             Leift: Coll: Cornelius Loyd)
             Major Thomas Lambert   ) Com'rs
             Capt: Xpfor Burrowgh   )

It is Ordered that Coll: Francis Yardley have the Command of the Company
which he formerly Commanded vizt: The Inhabitants of the Westerne
shoare of Lynhaven and the little Creeke, The families of Major Thomas
Lambert, Capt: X'pofer Burrough and Thomas Bridge gent Excepted. And
that Leift: Coll: Cornelius Loyd have the Command of the family of Capt:
Thomas Willoughby and all the Inhabitants from thence to the mouth of
the Easterne Branch of Elizabeth River, And all of the Inhabitants of
the Westerne branch, and the Westerne side of the Southerne Branch of
the said River, The family of Major Lambert Excepted. And that Major
Lambert hath the Command of all the rest of the Inhabitants of Elizabeth
River aforesaid, And of the three families Excepted out of Coll: Yardley
his former Company. And that Capt Xpofer Burrough have the Command of
the Inhabitants of the Easterne Shoare of Lynhaven River. And every one
of the said Commanders for the Malitia have power to appoint his officers
for the Exercaseinge of his owne Company And doe all things appointed by
Act of Assembly"

p.21   Order that ammunitions remain where they are. Also order concerning gun smith's work.

p.21   Coll: Francis Yardley ordered to collect 6 lb tobo per poll for
purchase of ammunition in which he has been delinquent.

p.21   Certificate for 300 acres to Francis Emperor for importing himself, Mary Emperor, Charles Emperor, Roose (or Reese) Joanes, Dannell
Mackfarson and Augustine Addeson.

1652

p.21   Ordered to be recorded 8 Oct 1652.
A judgt acknowledged before Henery Woodhouse, John Sidney and Lemuell
Mason, gent., Com'rs., by Coll Francis Yardley for paymt of 583 lb tobo
to John Piggott, merchant, it being a debt due from John Cornelius.

p.22.   Ordered to be recorded 15 Oct 1652.
Thos Knight confesses he owes Wm Basnett 3 bbl Indian corn. He is ordered to pay. Dated 13 Oct 1652.   Signed   Hen: Woodhouse

p.22   Ordered to be recorded 25 Oct 1652.
Richard Bennett, Esquire, Governor and Capt: Generall of Virginia,
appoints Commissioners for Lower Norfolk County.

                         Coll Francis Yardley
                         Leift: Coll: Cornelius Loyd
                         Mr Henry Woodhouse
                         Major Tho. Lambert
                         Leift: Coll: John Sidney
                         Mr: Will: Moseley
                         Mr: Lemuel Mason
                         Mr: William Daines
                         Mr: Christo: Burrough
                         Mr Francis Emperor
                         Mr Thomas Bridge
                         Mr Thomas Guttaridge   (Goodrich)

Dated 15 Oct. 1652
Signed   Will: Clauborne   Ri: Bennett

Coll: Francis Yardley, Leift: Coll: Cornelius Loyd, Major Thomas
Lambert and Mr Christo: Burrowgh "to have the power of the Militia".
                             Teste Rob: Huberd

p.23   A Court held 25 Oct 1652
       Present
          Mr Henery Woodhouse   Mr John Sidney
          Major Thomas Lambert   Mr Lemuel Mason   Com'rs.

p.23   Francis Land ordered to pay John Rabley assignee of Will: Westerhouse 2200 lb tobo due by bill. Robt Powes, atty of Land to pay from
Land's estate, he being out of the Colony.

p.23   John Lownes ordered to pay Jno Rabley 1300 lb tobo due by bill.

p.23   On petition of William Jermy, an order that Simond Overzee, mercht

pay 499 lb tobo to Jermy being a debt due from the est of Robt Eyre decd
for Clerk's fees. Overzee having formerly engaged himself in open Court
to pay in behalf of John Custis, mercht, who married the relict of Eyre.

p.23   John Lownes having arrested John Rabley to this Court and not
appearing is nonsuited.

p.23   Thos Bridge having arrested Geo Heigham to this Court and not
appearing is nonsuited.

p.23 The cause betw Geo Heigham pltf and Coll: Thomas Burbage deft ref
to next Court.

p.23   The cause betw Lewes Farmall plt and Jno Biggs ref to next Court.

p.23   Certificate for 150 acres to John Chandler for transporting himself, Edmund Magonnoe and Thomas Roth into this Colony.

p.23   By testimony of Thos Sayer, Anne Godby, contrary to Law, conducted
away the maid servant of Lewes Farmall. She fined 200 lb tobo.

p.23   Persons having estates of orphans ordered to make accounting in
Court.

p.23   On petition of John Carraway, he to have half of male increase of
a cow given by Richd Wester (or Woster) to the orphan of Roger Williams,
now in possession of sd Carraway who married the relict of Williams.
Carraway to bring a/c of the cattle to Court.

p.23   The fine of Wm Wilson for nonappearance at the house of Francis
Emperor, gent., is remitted, he having shown good cause for absence.
        Also the fine of Robt Yonge remitted in like.

p.24   Edward Wilder ordered to pay debt of corn to Wm Robinson, cooper.

p.24   On petition of Robt Davyes, he to have power to kill a bull about
7 years old belonging to the estate of the orphans of John May and now
in his custody. The bull to be valued by Jno Stratton and Edwd Cooper.
Davyes to also dispose of other cattle.

p.24   The cause betw Edwd Hall, chirurgeon, and Coll: Francis Yardley
referred to next Court.

p.24   Recorded 10 Nov. 1652.
William Harris and Company of Rotterdam, merchants, give a general
release from all debts, claims, etc., to Capt: Francis Yardley.
Dated 22 January 1650/51.
Wit: Signed   William Harris
Job: Chandler
Simon Overzee

p.24   Recorded 10 Nov 1652.
"I William Moseley late of Rotterdam in Holland in the partes beyond the
seaes March't: And now resident and inhabittinge in the Easterne branch
of Elizabeth River in the County of Lower Norfolk" being "possessed of
certeine peeces of Gouldsmyths and Juellers worke to the valewe of Six
hundred and twelve Gilders As namely One hatband consisting of Nineteene Ses of gould, Nineteene Ies of gould, one buckle and tipp of gould
all sett with Dyamonds and in part Enamelled Att five hundred gilders,
one Juell of gould Enamelled and sett with Diamonds Att sixty gilders
and one gould Ringe enamelled and sett with one Diamon, one Rubie one
sapher and one Emrall Att Fifty two gilders" have this day sold to Capt
Francis Yardley of Linhaven "the said hatband, Juell and Ringe" for 9
head of cattle. The cattle were "Two draught Oxen two steeres and five
Cowes in hand already received". Dated 1 August 1650.
Wit: Signed   William Moseley
Edward Windhām
Edw: Standley

p.24
    "Worthy Sir
    My husband havinge some bussiness downe the river was gone from home
two horrows before your servant came soe I findinge what the contents of
your letter did import, have in my husbands absence made bould to answer
it and withall I knowe he referrs the sale of them to me Sir in regarde
you cannot out of your stocke no meer then fower younge Cowes and one
older and fower exen I will not press you beyond what you are willinge
to doe, but will accept of your proffer, by reason of my greate wante of
Cattle, and withall I had rayther your wife should weare them than aney
gentlewoman I yet know in the Country, but good Sir, have no Scruple
Concerninge theire rightnes for I went my selfe from Rotterdam to the
Haguh, to inquire of the gouldsmiths and found that they weare all Right
therfore thats without question, and for the hatband that alone coste
five hundred gelders as my husband knows verry well and will tell you
soe when he sees you, for the Juell and the ringe they weare made for
me at Rotterdam and I paid in good Rex Dollores for them sixtey gelders

for the Jewell and fivety and two gelders for the Ringe, Which comes to
in English monny Eleaven pounds fower shillings. I have sent the sute,
and Ringe by your servant and I wish Mrs Yeardley health and prosperity
to weare them in and give you boeth thanks for your kinde token. When
my husband come home we will see to gett the Cattell home in the meane
time I present my love and service to your selfe and wife. Mr Chandler
and his wife and the younge gentlewoman and old Cap't. and Commit you all
to god

                                     and remaine your freind and
Elizabeth River this   servant:
Last July 1650:   Susan Moseley   "

Recorded 10th November 1652.

Note: Of the Moseleys much has been written. Their portraits, now
distributed, were said to be the handsomest collection in America. I
count among my friends the present day son and heir, Mr. Grandison
Moseley, who lived half a block from me in an enormous old house. There
have been times when I would have just loved to crack him over the
knuckles with a ruler. He is rather frail and delicate although his
behavior, and that of his brother Tom,has not always been that. He is
known among the fellows here in Richmond as "Granny".   B.F.

p.25. Recorded 10 Nov 1652.
Thos Allen of Linhaven in the Co of Lower Norfolk, planter, releases Col
Francis Yardley of the same place from all debts, claims, etc.
Dated 1 May 1652.   Signed   Tho: Allen
Wit:
Edward Windham
John Rice

p.25   Recorded 10 Nov 1652.
        A Court for Elizabeth City 17 Nov 1651.
        Present   Capt Tho Ceeley   )
                   Major Wm Worlick) Comrs   Mr Humphrey Tabb
                   Mr John Chandler)

Thos Edmunds acks judgt for 1013 lb tobo due Thomas Godwyn. He to pay
in 10 days.   Henery Poole   Clerk of Court

(Poole was Clerk in Elizabeth City County as far back as 1640. B.F.)

1652

p.25   A Court 2 Nov 1652. Lower Norfolk Co.
        Present
                Leift: Coll: Cornelius Loyd   Mr X'pofer Burrowes
                Major Tho: Lambert   Mr Thomas Bridge
                Mr Francis Emperor   Com'rs

p.25   On pet of Wm Daynes, gent., "that the poore and inconsiderate
Estate left by Thomas Lewes deceased, whereby to take L'res of Adminis-
tracon would much consume the said estate". Order that Robt Grimes who
was partner with Lewes take all the estate and pay the debts.

p.25   Major Tho Lambert makes it appear that Ellis Browne illegally
transported Wm Stone out of this Colony. That Stone owes him 900 lb tobo.
Attachmt agst est of Browne for this amt.

p.25   The Court to be adjourned to 10 Dec after the meeting of the
Assembly to avoid expense and "other reasons too tedious to relate".

p.26   A Court held 10 Dec 1652.
        Present
                Leift: Coll: Cornelius Loyd   Mr Thomas Bridge
                Mr Henery Woodhouse   Major Tho: Lambert
                Mr Christopher Burrowes   Com'rs

p.26   Rowland Morgan to pay debt of 300 lb tobo due Jno Holmes assignee
of Thos Woodward.

p.26   "John Cubbidge and Stephen Key (or Rey ?) have accordinge to Act
of Assembly sett upp their names at the Court house dore givinge notice
of their intended voyage for England this present Shipping".

p.26   Attachmt granted Left: Cornelius Loyd for 550 lb tobo agst the est
of Peter Garnitent (or Garnitout ?)

p.26   Court adjourned to 21 December.

1652

p.26   A Court 21 Dec 1652
        Present
            Left: Coll: Cornelius Loyd   Mr Lemuell Mason
            Mr Henery Woodhouse   Mr Francis Emperor
            Major Thomas Lambert   Mr Thomas Bridge   Com'rs

p.26   Letters of Admr to Jno Richards on est of Even Willetts as the
greatest creditor.

p.26   On pet of Jane Rigglesworth, widow, she to be pd debts from est
of Even Willetts

p.26   Jno Richards, admr of Even Willetts decd, ordered to pay debt of
242 lb tobo due James Frisbye from the est. Also tp pay Lt Col Cornelius
Loyd—300 lb tobo due from the est. The estate to be sold at public outcry 6 Jan and Jane Riglesworth to produce goods in her possession.

p.26   Certificate for 200 acres to Jane Riglesworth, widow, for importing: Jane Williams   Charles Mograth
                John Tutte   Mary Gutter

p.26   Probate to Jane Riglesworth of the will of Peter Riglesworth decd
her late husband, she being sole extrx.

p.27   Dif betw Wm Robinson pltf and Jno Martin deft to next Court.

p.27   Jno Williams ordered to pay debt of 160 lb tobo due to Thomas
Buckmaster assignee of Geo Johnson.
Also to pay Francis Emperor gent atty for Thos Marsh 229 lb tobo due him.

p.27   Dif betw Wm Merritt pltf and James Thelabell deft to next Court.
Also dif betw Tho Ward pltf and Thelabell deft to next Court.

p.27   Dif betw George Kemp plt and Wm Moseley gent deft to next Court.

p.27   Dif betw Thos Daynes atty of Cornelius Bonner and John Lownes deft
to next Court.

p.27   "More present Leift Coll: John Sidney"

p.27   Christopher Rivers ordered to pay debt of 700 lb tobo and 4 bbl Indian corn due John Lownes, gent.

p.27 Peter Sexton ordered to pay debt of 1522 lb tobo due Fr: Emperor as atty of Tho Marsh.

p.27   Dif betw Thos Dadford pltf and Deborah the wife of Geo Heigham deft to next Court.

p.27   In dif betw Wm Moseley plt and Jno Lownes concerning the sale of a negro and "findinge the said Lownes to be guilty of false premisses made to the said Moseley" in regard to the soundness of the negro, Lownes to pay Moseley 1200 lb tobo. Lownes appeals to the Genl Court. Major Tho Lambert goes his security.

p.27   Dif betw Geo Heigham plt and Capt Tho Burbage deft to next Court.

p.27   Dif betw Tho Daynes Atty of Richd Pinner pltf and Major Thomas Lambert deft to next Court.
Also: Dif betw Daynes and Elizabeth Sibsey to next Court.

p.27   Robt Woody to pay debt 500 lb tobo due Mathew Howard.

p.27   Certificate for 350 acres to George Ashall for transporting

Richard Walker	Thomas Choswell
Leven Butler	John Banks
Raffe Synes	Wm Panyer
Mary Storey	

p.27   Certificate to Robt Capps for 200 acres for transporting

Himself	Isabel Hingle
Robte Springe	John Gregman

p.27   Certificate for 300 acres to John Hatton for transporting

John Harris	James Jenkins
Edmond Yeomans	X'pfor Vaughan
John Searle	Thomas Atkinson

p.28   Admr of est of Tho Tooker decd to Lt Col Cornelius Loyd as the greatest creditor. This with consent of Dorothy Tooker late wife of Tho Tooker.

p.28   The following to be paid debts due from the estate of Thos Tooker.
Leift: Coll John Sidney, amt not shown.
Thomas Browne   972 lb tobo.
James Frisbye, gent.,   776 lb tobo.
Richard Sternell,   757--lb tobo.
Laurence Phillipps,   1671 lb tobo.

p.28   Admr of estate of Capt Mathew Wood decd to Thomas Goodrich, gent.

p.28   On petition of Robt Powes, order that Thos Keelinge, John Martin,
Simon Cornix and Owen Hayes appraise the estate of Robt Powes, Clerk,
deceased, and report to next Court.

Note: Robert Powis, Minister of Lynnhaven Parish, Lower Norfolk Co.
from about 1645 to his death in 1652.   B.F.

p.28   Jno Williams to pay 358 lb tobo due Thos Daynes atty of Geo Mee.

p.28   Robt Hogborne ordered to pay damages to Lemuell Mason gent for
opening a hhd of tobo.

p.28   Certificate for 550 acres to Richd Sternell for transportation of
11 persons into this Colony, vizt:
      By himself 4 persons
                     Richard Tompson   Daniell Pulson
                     Richard Joanes   John Rey
      And by assignment of John Lownes
                     Wm Eale   Henery Lambert
                     George Gosden   Mary Gouldsmith
                     Mary a Negro   John Lownes and his wife

p.28   Mr Mason and Mr Lambert absent.

p.28   On petition of Wm Moseley, gent, execution to be stayed on order
granted agst him at suit of Jno Lownes, gent, for 1000 lb tobo until
another suit betw them, appealed to James City be settled.

p.28   Present Mr Lambert and Mr Mason.
        (They must have just stepped out to get a drink. B.F.)

p.28   Dif betw John Hill pltf and Wm Johnson deft to next Court.

p.28   According to an order made in the last Assembly at James Citty,
Mr Francis Emperor was this-day sworn Surveyor for this Colony of
Virginia.   (21 December 1652).

p.29   In cause depending at James City ref to this Court, upon petition
of John Mendham, admr of Thos Leech dec'd, order that Mr Henery Woodhouse sell all hogs belonging to Leech and Jno Newman in their lifetime
and take care of the cattle and other goods, and report to next Court.

p.29   Order that Mr Jno Piggott receive all bills delivered this Court
by Jno Custis who married the relict of Robt Eyre dec'd, and Simon
Overzee merchant belonging to the estate of Eyre. Piggott to give a/c
to this Court on demand.
A list of bills: Mr Brice   450 lb tobo
                     Edward Standley   252   "
                     Mr Piggott his note   136   "
                     Thomas Cartwright   164   "
                     Mr John Sidney   502   "
                     Simond Handcooke   180   "
                     Mr Spry   2000   "
                                             - - - -
                                             3684

p.29   Certificate for 50 acres to Bartholomewe Hoskins for transporting
Thomas Rentinge (or Kentinge ?) into this Colony. This assigned to
Hoskins by Jno Cooke decd in his lifetime.

p.29   Dif betw Geo Fletcher atty of Capt William Douglas and Company,
pltf, vs Lemuell Mason, gent, referred to next Court.

p.29   Order that the Sheriff levy for Coll: Wm Clayborne, 1000 lb tobo
from the estate of Wm Moseley, gent, "beinge for arreeares left unpaid
in the yere 1650".

p.29   Geo Johnson ordered to pay debt of 370 lb tobo due Mary Page.

p.29   On petition of Andrewe Michells "setting forth the abuse of John
Davyes towards him by stricking and beatinge the said Michells in a most
pittifull manner, and the said Michells being an aged man, And fully
provinge the same in open Court uppon oath", order that Davyes at the
expiration of the term he has to serve to Capt Thos Willoughby, serve
Michells 6 months or pay him 600 lb tobo.

p.29   George Heigham ordered to pay debt of 500 lb tobo due Tho Bridge.

p.29   Quietus est to Thos Sawyer, admr of Stephen Hix dec'd, having
fully discharged himself and "by a generall release under the hand of
Henery Barlowe Attorney of Judith Hix als Brice of Southampton in
England mother of the said Stephen Hix".

p.29   In dif betw Tho Godby pltf and Tho Spill deft, upon full hearing
in Court, Godby ordered to pay Spill 28 lb tobo for Court charges, and
also 40 lb tobo for 3 days attendence at Court "And in respect of the
said Godbye his unjust malefac'on ag't the said Spill".

p.29   Certif for 100 acres to Tho Hall for transporting Owen Daniell
and John Kelson (or Relson ?).

p.29   Tho Davis to pay debt of 379 lb tobo due Major Lambert.

p.29   Attachmt to Major Thos Lambert for 3626 lb tobo due him from the
estate of Geo Heigham, also for 688 lb tobo due from Clement Theoballs
and also for 1274 lb tobo due from Peter Grantor

p.30   The Sheriff ordered to bring Rowland Morgan to Court at the suit
of Major Tho: Lambert.
Also to bring John Hill at Lambert's suit.

p.30   The next Court to be held 17th January 1652/3.

p.30   Certificate for 50 acres to John Godfrey for transportation of
Allexander Gwinn into this Colony. Ordered to be recorded 21 Dec 1652.

p.30   22 December 1651 (sic). Receipt from Henery Barlowe, atty of
Judith Hix als Brice of Southampton, for 2000 lb tobo for use of Robte
Brice, marriner, and his wife Judith Hix als Brice, in full satisfaction
of "an Estate of Stephen Hix deceased in Virginia in the yere 1648".
Received by Barlowe from Mr Thomas Sawyer "as witnes my hand beinge
resident in Elizabeth River in the County of Lower Norffolke in Virginia"
Wit: Signed   Henery Barlowe
Richard Pinner
John Bigge

p.30 Will of Peter Riglesworth. Dated 2 Sept 1652. Recorded 21 Dec 1652.
To wife, Jane, and 2 children, stock to be div equally betw them. Daus
    Mary and Dorothy, both under 16 and unmarried. Land to wife, 500 lb
    tobo to each dau.
To John Beymus (sic) son of John Beymous (sic) a cow.
To John Tutt "my servant" a cow about 3 yrs hence. To remain in custody
    of wife till Tutt be free.
To Charles Morgan "my servant", if he serve out his time without trouble,
    "my best suite of Cloathes besides his freedome cloathes"
Overseers: Charles Stevens, Robte Bowers and Robte Capps.
To Robte Capps and Robte Springe perfect assurance of land sold them.
Wit: Signed   the marke of
Robte Springe   Peter x Riglesworth
Even x Willetts
John Finch
-
All 3 witnesses swear he intended to make his wife Extrx, but the words
were neglected.

p.30   Deed. 17 Dec 1649. Richd Yates sells Thos Horne land, acerage not
shown. Betw 2 branches beginning at the River side, and being in the
Southern branch of the Elizabeth River, being the land the sd Thomas
Horne is now seated on, etc.
Wit: Signed   Richard x Yates
John Finch
John Wilkinson   Sealed and delivered 29 Oct 1652.

p.31   Recorded 21 Dec 1652.
Inv of Est of Robte Powes, Clerk, deceased, now in possession of Robte
Powes, his son, exor. The items not valued.
Includes:
It'm two suites of Cloathes and three Coates and two Cassacks
It'm Two and thirty bookes

p.31
Lower Norff'
The 21 day of December Anno d'm 1652 the particular accompts and paymts
to be made out of the County Levyes for this present yere, vizt.
-   lb tobo
To the Publique   9729
To Leift: Coll: Cornelius Loyd for beinge Burgesse 3
    Assemblyes   4150
To Major Thomas Lambert for Three Assemblyes   2500
To Mr Woodhouse one Assembly   1385
To John Martin for one Assembly   0700
                        (continued)

1652

	lb tobo
To Mr X'pofer Burroughs for three Assemblyes	2500
To Mrs Burroughs for one Wolfe killinge	0100
To mr Hoskins for one Assembly	0400
To him more for provission for the Burgesses at James towne	0325
To mr William Daynes high Shereive by account	2014
To mr Lownes for dyet for the Burgesses at James towne	0070
To Mathewe Howard for killinge one wolfe	0100
To Thomas Dadford for the like and by account	0190
To Lancaster Lovett for the like	0190
To Francis Emperor gent for his boate hire	0120
To John Clarke 25: dayes at 10 lb the day	0250
To mr Conquest 19 dayes for his man at 10 lb the day	0190
To Gyles Collins for killinge one wolfe	0100
To George Kempe 23: dayes for his man	0230
To Laurence Phillipps by account	0321
To James Phillipps Eleaven dayes	0110
To X'pofer Smith for killinge two wolves	0200
To John Dyer Eleaven Dayes	0110
To James Lopham his attendance at James towne	0572
To John Stratton for boate hire	0150
To George Johnson	0020
To Addam Hayes hire to James Towne	0300
To John Rabley for his boate to James towne	0500

```
To Sallery for 27526: at 10 per Cent   3231
                    For Overplus        0573   lb tob:
                    Sum total          31330
```

p.32
"For satisfacon of theforesaid Some of Thirty one thousand Three hundred
and Thirty pounds of tobacco, It is Ordered there be Levied of everye
Tytheable person within this County beinge according to the list given
in fower hundred Eighty and two persons at sixty five pounds of tobacco
per poll: amounts unto the some of 31330 lb of tobacco, beinge Overplus
573 lb of tobacco"

Leift: Colli Cornelius Loyd to be Collector for the Western Branch in
Elizabeth River from 97 tytheable persons. And to pay as follows:

To Sallery	0742
To himselfe by account	4150
To mr Woodhouse	0350
To Mathewe Howard	0100
To mr William Daynes Heigh Shreive	0963

	6305

(continued next page)

1652

Accounts for the County, 1652 (continued)

p.32   Major Thos Lambert Collector for Eastern and Southern branches
in Elizabeth River from 117 tytheables.

To Sallery	0872
To his own account	2500
To mr Hoskins	0725
To mr William Daynes	1051
To Thomas Dadford	0190
To Francis Emperor gent	0120
To George Kempe	0230
To Richard Conquest gent	0190
To Laurence Phillipps	0321
To Sir William Berkeley	0621
To mr Corker	0785
	7605

p.32   Mr Thomas Bridge Collector for the Little Creeks from 82 tytheable persons

To Sallery	0645
To John Clarke	0250
To John Dyer	0110
To James Lopham	0572
To mr John Lownes	0070
To Gyles Collins	0100
To George Johnson	0020
To Addam Hayes	0360
To mr Corker	3263
	5330

p.32   Mr John Sidney Collector for the Eastern Shore of Lynnhaven from
63 tytheables

To Sallery	0521
To Mr Woodhouse	1035
To James Phillipps	0110
To John Rabley	0500
To Coll: Floudd	1929
	4095

(continued next page)

Accounts for the County, 1652 (continued)

p.32   Mr Lemuell Mason Collector from Daniell Tanner's Creeke to Capt
Willoughbyes from 45 tytheables.

To Sallery	0404
To mr William Jermy	1500
To X'pofer Smith	0200
To John Stratton	0150
To Lancaster Lovett	0190
To Coll Flood	0481
	2925

p.32   Francis Emperor Collector for the Western Shore of Lynnhaven,
78 tytheables.

To Sallery	0620
To mr Xpofer Burroughs	2600
To John Martin	0700
To Coll Flood	0577
per Overplus	0573
	5070

Sum total 31330 lb of tob
per Willm Jermy   Clerk

. . . .

p.33   Lower Norfolk. A Court 17 January 1652/3.
      Present
            Collo Francis Yardley   Mr Lemuell Mason
            Leift: Coll: Cornelius Loyd   Mr Francis Emperor
            Major Thomas Lambert   Mr Thomas Bridge
            Leift: Coll: John Sidney   Mr Thomas Goodrich   Com'rs

p.33   Probate of will of Samuell Charinose, decd, to Wm Jacob, the
whole estate left to him.

p.33   Dif betw Tho Davis pltf and Edwd Wilder deft ref to next Court.

p.33   In dif betw Thos Daynes pltf and John White deft, that if White
did not appear and show the Court that Daynes was pd 845 lb tobo, "under
the hand of one Jeremy Ham", that White was to pay. This by the oath of
George Kempp. Daynes further claimed 477 lb tobo due him from White by
assignment from Thomas Edmonds.

p.33   Judgt ack by Peter Knight mercht for paymt of 1200 lb tobo with
4 years forbearance (interest) to Tho Bridge gent.

p.33   On petition of "Allexander make Allestre" it is ordered that he
be free, being acknowledged by Elizabeth Sibsey the relict of Capt John
Sibsey "whom he hath served". She to give him "One kersey suite two
shirts two paire of Shooes two paire of Stockings and Corne" according
to custom.
Note: WHAT is this entry ? However true, I simply decline to believe
any such thing !   B.F.

p.33   Order that all dif betw Jno Richards and Jane Riglesworth, widow,
re the est of Even Willetts be referred to 13 Feb next. Then to be heard
and determined by Leift: Coll: Cornelius Loyd, Major Tho Lambert and Fr.
Emperor, gent, at the house of Thomas Goodrich, gent.

p.33   Jno Richards admr of Even Willetts to pay 1056 lb tobo due, with
interest, to Richard Bennett Esqr.

p.33   Judgt ack by Peter Garnitente and Wm Jacob for paymt of 800 lb
tobo due Lt Col Cornelius Loyd on 10 Oct next "uppon forfeite of their
whole Estates in case of non payment".

p.33   Order that Lt Col Jno Sidney, Mr Tho Bridge, Mr Edwd Hall sen'r
and Mr Tho Keetinge appraise the est of Christopher Burroughs, gent,
deceased, upon 3 Feb next "at the house of Mary Burrowes wid' And mr
Henery Woodhouse is requested to be then and there present".

p.33   Admr of est of Christopher Burroughs "her late husband" to Mary
Burroughs, widow.

p.33   In dif betw Wm Robinson and John Martin, order that Robinson set
up all such casks as are left by him, according to agreemt, the profits
to be divided and Martin to give an a/c at next Court.

p.33   In dif betw Moyses Linton pltf and Francis Emperor deft. Emperor
ordered to furnish Linton with a sufficient man servant "at the next
arrivall of English Shipping heere that brings in servants to be sould"

p.33   Tho Wethell atty of Peter King having arrested Col Fr. Yardley
to this Court and not appearing is nonsuited.

p.34   On petition of Wm Daynes atty of John Jasperson, an attachmt is
granted him on est of Wm Westerhouse in the hands of Thomas Daynes for
10250 lb tobo. Westerhouse being out of this County.

p.34   Quietus est to Robte Powes on est of his father Robte Powes deod.

p.34   Order that Mary Savill, admrx of Jno Cooke, pay 270 lb tobo due
in lifetime of Cooke to Major Tho Lambert. Also to pay Robt Powes 500
lb tobo due him.

p.34   Dif betw Richd Joanes pltf and Jno Lownes gent to next Court.

p.34   Dif betw Richd Chapman plt and Jno Lownes deft to next Court.

p.34   Certif for 100 acres to Jno Bigge for transporting Johan Bigge
and Joseph Hutt into this Colony.

p.34   Judgt ack by Edw: Wilder for paymt of 1015 lb tobo to Geo Heigham

p.34   Geo Heigham ordered to pay 870 lb tobo to Edward Wilder due "for
Stayne Worke".   (Painting ?)

p.34   Edward Wilder fined 50 lb tobo for swearing in Court.
        (Evidently he was a painter !)

p.34   In dif betw Geo Heigham pltf and Coll: Tho Burbage, if Burbage
fails to appear at next Court Judgt to go agst him.

p.34   Lt Col Cornelius Loyd, admr of Tho Tooker deod, ordered to pay
400 lb tobo due Job Chandler gent.

p.34   Certificate for 1250 acres to Tho Goodrich, gent, for transporting 13 persons into this Colony, 9 of them assigned over to Peter Sexton
in open Court, vizt: himself, Anne his wife and 7 negroes. Other names
not shown in the record.

p.34   James Thelaball to pay 2 bbl corn due to Wm Merritt.

1652/3

p.34   Lt Col Cornelius Loyd, admr of est of Tho Tooker, to pay 37? lb tobo due Richd Sternell.

p.34   Dif betw Edwd Hall, chirurgeon, and Wm Robinson referred to hearing of Mr Jno Sidney and Mr Tho Bridge at the house of Mr Sidney the 1st of Feb next.

p.34   On petition of Tho Lambert, gent, the dif betw Jno Robins pltf, Admr of Wm Moore, decd, and Elizabeth Sibsey, widow, extrx of Capt Jno Sibsey, decd, referred to next Court.

p.34   In dif betw Tho Ward and James Thelaball, order that Thelaball hold and enjoy that Neck of Land he has now seated, which is a part of lease land lying in Woolves Neck formerly demised unto Thos Ward by Leift Coll Cornelius Loyd as agent for the orphan of Henery Hawkins. Thelaball to pay 700 lb tobo to Ward.

p.34   On petition of Peter Grintoe, he to be free from taxes "being very aged and past his Labour".

p.35   In a former dif betw Timothy Ives pltf and Richd Trewe deft, Trewe being arrested, Tho Lambert gent became his bail. Trewe not appearing, Lambert confessed judgt for 624 lb tobo. Trewe being then and now out of the Colony, an order the judgt be voided.

p.35   Attachmt to Laurence Phillipps agst the est of Robte Taylor for 447 lb tobo. Taylor being out of this County no judgt to pass until he is notified.

p.35   Stephen Key (or Rey ?) to be pd 975 lb tobo from est of John Cooke decd by Mary Savill Admrx.

p.35   That Geo Fletcher admr of Capt Wm Douglas having impleaded Lemuell Mason gent concerning debts due from the est of Henery Sewell gent decd, and also a maid servant, Mason to pay, etc., etc.

p.35   That Edward Cannon got his maid servant with child long before his marriage to her, is fined 600 lb tobo.
Note: We can understand the shotgun marriage, but this sort of minding another man's business, this interference with his most private affairs is beyond the comprehension of the modern mind.   B.F.

p.35 In dif betw Tho. Dadford pltf and Deborah the wife of Geo Heigham déft there to be a hearing before Major Tho Lambert and Lt Col John Sidney on the 2nd of Feb at the home of Sidney.

p.35 That Capt Jno Sibsey, in his lifetime, owed Stephen Gearoy 1700 lb tobo, yet unpd. Elizabeth Sibsey the extrx to pay Mr Richd Pinner atty of Gearoy 700 lb tobo in part settlement.

p.35 An attachmt granted Edward Gunnell, marriner, agst the est of Stephen Gearoy in hands of Capt Jno Sibsey.

p.35 Dif betw Richd Chapman plt vs Tho Lambert gent ref to next Court.

p.35 Richd Richardson mercht pltf vs Thos Lambert gent appealed to Genl Court by Lambert.

p.35 Dif betw Richard Richardson plt and Mathewe Fassett deft, Fassett to pay 500 lb tobe and further a hhd of tobo "lyeinge at one Garretts house and received by one mr Bacon" net wt 381 lb tobo to be made good by Fassett to Richardson if Richardson makes proof of ownership.

p.36 Dorothy Tooker, widow, relict of Tho Tooker deed, ordered to give in inventory of the est to Mr Tho Goodrich, Com'r.

p.36 Jno Holmes ordered to pay 1539 lb tobo and 3 years forbearance (interest) to Tho Bridge gent who married the relict of Mathewe Phillipps dec'd.

p.36 Attachmt to Mary Burroughs, widow and admrx of Christopher Burroughs gent, deed, for 285 lb tobo agst the est of Jno Cornelius in the hands of Wm Fann.

p.36 Attachmt to Coll Wm Clayborne for debt due (amt not shown) agt est of Richard Hill

p.36 The Sheriff ordered to produce Robt Taylor who was arrested at suit of Col Wm Clayborne and did not appear.
Also attachmt to Col Clayborne agst the estate of Bartholomewe Rench for debt due and agst the est of Tobias Mathewes.

p.36   An Orphans Court to be held 17th Feb next at house of Laurence
Phillipps.

p.36   Certif for 100 acres to John Sidney, gent, for transporting
Thos Everard and Bridgett Ellenor into this Colony.

p.36   Certif for 200 acres to John Porter for transporting Sarah Smith,
Robte Peacock, Daniell Douglas and Daniel Macklude into this Colony.

p.36   "17th January 1652 Ordered to be Recorded"
"George Hawkins is this day fined One hundred pounds of tobacco for
takinge a Jugge out of Lynhaven Church, beinge left there for the
prishioners use, to be disposed of at the discretion of the next Court
to be houlden for this County Dated this 13th day of January Ao Dm
1652"

                            Signed   Fran: Yardley)
                                       John Sidney   ) Com'rs
                                       Tho Bridge   )

p.36   17 Jan 1652/3.
        Owen Hayes records mark for cattle and hogs.
        Wm Robinson   "
        Tho Keeling   "

p.36   Will of Samuell Charnicoe (or Jarmicoe).
Dated 13 Dec 1652. Recorded 17 Jan 1652/3.
His daughter Rose Charnicoe (sic) "I doe putt forth" unto Wm Jacob for
        term of 16 years.
"I doe putt forth Edward Rutland" to said Wm Jacob for term of 21 years.
To Wm Jacob a cow and a heifer on the ground of Edward Cooper. Also the
        venture of a hhd of tobo sent to England by Thos Allen.
Wit: Signed   the marke of
Tobias Mathewes   Samuell x Jarmicoe   (sic)
John Clarke

p.36   "The Deposicon of Tobias Mathewes aged 35 yeres or thereabouts"
Says this is the last will of Samuell Charnicoe. Dated 16 Jan 1652/3.
Wit: Signed   Tobias Mathewes
Henery Woodhouse

p.37   Inventory of estate of Robt Powes, Clerk. Totals 11620 lb tobo.
Recorded 17 Jan 1652/3   Signed   Leift Keelinge)
                                         Henery Snayle) their markes
                                         Owen Hayes   )
                                         John Martin

1652/3

p.37   Account of tobo Stephen Key (or Rey ?) "disbursed for the use
of John Cooke deceased". Total 5975 lb tobo: Includes:

To mr Odeon for a servant	1500
To mr Meares	1400
To Thomas Hall	0100
To mr Bosworth for knives	0252
To John Workeman for washinge	0070
To Thomas Workeman	0250
More due to me for tobacco laid out when John Cooke was in England	0973

Sworn in Court 17 Jan 1652/3

p.37   Roger Fountayne ordered to pay Richd Smith 910 lb tobo.
Dated 4 Feb 1652/3   Signed   Tho Lambert   )
                                             Fran: Emperor)   Com'rs
                                             Tho Bridge   )

p.37   Edw Wilder ordered to pay Geo Heigham 295 lb tobo.
Dated 3 Feb 1652/3   Signed   Tho: Lambert)
                                             John Sidney   )   Com'rs

p.37   3rd Feb 1652/3. In dif betw Tho Dadford pltf and Deborah, wife of
Geo Heigham, deft, Heigham to pay charges and Deborah to ack her fault.
                                    Signed   Tho Lambert
                                             John Sidney

p.37   On petition of Mary Burrowes, widow, admrx of Christo: Burrowes
dec'd, the estate to be appraised by Lt Col Jno Sidney, Mr Tho Bridge,
Ensigne Thos Keelinge and Mr Edwd Hall. That Lt Col Jno Sidney failing
to appear "of badnesse and tediousnes of the weather" Wm Robinson to
be put in his place. 4 Feb 1652/3   Signed   Tho Lambert)
                                               Fran: Emperor)   Com'rs

p.37   Tho Horne records mark for cattle and hogs. 16 Feb 1652/3.
                                    Signed   Wm Jermy   Clerk

p.38   Simon Peeters "aged about Two and forty yeeres" swears that about
5 yrs since, living at the house of Mr Phillipps, Mr Plott came thither
and being in discourse about a maid servant named Katherine Preisthood,
he offered the maid to Phillipps for 1000 lb tobo. That Phillipps offered 700 lb tobo which was taken. Some other detail, etc.
                                    Signed   Simon x Peeters
Sworn 16 Feb 1652/3.

p.38   Recorded 16 Feb 1652/3. Deed. Andrew Warner sells Edw Cannon
and Tho Allen a parcel of land. This entry does not show what or where.
Dated 1st Dec 1651.   Signed   Andrewe Warner
Wit:
Wm Lucas
Isacke Morgan
Memo: "theabovsd bill of sale Recorded the 12th day of August Ao: 1647"

p.38   Recorded 16 Feb 1652/3.
Abraham Thomas assigns right and title in a patent to Tho. Watkins.
Dated 16 Nov 1652.   Signed   Abraham x Thomas
Wit:
John Sidney
Willi: x Wilson
Also assigns int in 60 acres to above land. surveyed but not patented.

p.38   A Court 16 Feb 1652/3.
            Present
                Coll: Francis Yardley   Mr Lemuell Mason
                Left: Coll: Cornelius Loyd   Mr Francis Emperor
                Major Thomas Lambert   Mr Thomas Bridge
                Leift: Coll: John Sidney   Mr Thomas Goodrich

p.38   John Rabley fined 200 lb tobo for swearing 2 oaths in Court.

p.38   Dif betw Jno Robins admr of -- Moore decd, and Eliz Sibsey widow
and extrx of Capt Jno Sibsey, on petition of Lemuell Mason atty of Robins
is ref to next Court.

p.38   Dif betw Nathaniell Hayes pltf and Margarett the wife of William
Hatterfley referred to next Court.

p.38   Dif betw Mathewe Fassett pltf and Mary Saville Admrx of John
Cooke dect ref to next Court.

p.38   Dif betw Tho Edmonds pltf and Francis Emperor gent referred to
next Court.

p.38   Dif betw George Kempe pltf and Markes Leonard deft referred to
next Court.

p.38   Dif betw Col Francis Yardley pltf and John Lownes gent deft, in regard to a debt of 2400 lb tobo according to an agreement made 3rd March 1650/1, appealed to the Genl Court.
Also another case in which Major Thomas Lambert is security for Lownes appearance.

p.39   Thos Willoughby Junior ordered to pay Jno Rabley 2747 lb tobo on verdict of Jury and upon Court Order dated 15 Feb 1650/51.

p.39   Order that Geo Heigham pay Court charges of 243 lb tobo in former case of Tho Dadford pltf vs Deborah wife of Geo Heigham heard before Major Tho Lambert and Lt Col Jno Sidney.

p.39   Richd Sternell ordered to pay 880 lb tobo to Richd Chapman, atty of Barbara Hobson widow, due the estate of Capt Wm Hobson her late decd husband.

p.39   Jno Richards admr of est of Even Willett dec'd ordered to pay 140 lb tobo due John Finch.

p.39   At a Court held 15 Apl last past an attachmt was granted Simond Overzee agst the est of Wm Jaines dec'd for 1770 lb tobo. The attachment was served on 1400 lb tobo in hands of Mr Job Chandler, etc.

p.39   Tho Edwards to pay Thos Daynes gent 500 lb tobo for a boat he lost

p.39   Geo Heigham to pay John Marshall 1050 lb tobo in goods. The goods to be appraised by John Piggott mercht and Geo Kempe at the house of Heigham. Marshall to deliver a patent for land, etc.

p.39   Simon Overzee to pay 200 lb tobo to James Lopham for sending him on a voyage to James Town to carry letters to Leift: Coll: Childes.

p.39   Dif betw Tho Goodrich admr of Capt Mathewe Wood decd, pltf, and John Lownes regarding the estate, appealed to the Genl Court. Major Tho Lambert goes security for Lownes.

p.39   Gregory Parrett ordered to pay Edmund Bowman mercht 590 lb tobo due him.

p.39   "Whereas Francis Emperor Attorny of Thomas Marsh Sued Robte Grimes" for 481 lb tobo "which suite the said Grimes pleaded the Act of Assembly"

p.39   Attachmt to Col Francis Yardley agst est of Edw Standley dec'd in hands of Jno Martin for 875 lb tobo.

p.39   That Coll: Thos Burbage bought a tract of land from Robte Glaskooke dec'd now in possession of Wm Daynes gent. On petition of George Heigham who married the relict of said Glaskooke, Burbage to settle with him.

p.40   Dif betw Robt Porter and Richd Becke dismissed, each to pay the other's Court charges.

p.40   Jno Lownes ordered to pay Richd Joanes 100 lb tobo "for his unjust molestacon towards his Chardges".

p.40   Simond Overzee to pay Jno Piggott mercht 1569 lb tobo in full of all accounts due by Overzee from the estate of Robt Eyre gent decd, and in full discharge of Jno Custis who married the relict of Eyre.

p.40   Dif betw Richd Sternell and Tho Godby dismissed.

p.40   Eliz Sibsey widow and extrx of Capt John Sibsey to pay Edward Major gent L 10. Sterling due from Capt Sibsey in his lifetime.

p.40   In dif betw Wm Robinson pltf and Samuell Ruttland deft, in regard to Ruttland living with Robinson, order that Ruttland pay Robinson 100 lb tobo from the next crop.

p.40   Whereas Thomas Ward who married Alice the daughter of John Holmes petitioned this Court against Tho Bridge gent, who married the relict of Mathewe Phillipps dec'd, for satisfaction of certain goats given Ward's wife by Henery Sewell gent dec'd. Bridge to pay Ward 100 lb tobo in full discharge.

p.40   "Uppon the peticon of Dorothy Tooker widow setting forth the greate Chardge and Expence she was forced to disburse about the funerall of Thomas Tooker her late deceased husband", she to be paid from the estate by the Administrator.   (Cornelius Loyd, admr.)

p.40 Leift: Coll: Cornelius Loyd admr of Thos Tooker to pay 145 lb tobo due Mary Burrowes admrx of X'pofer Burrowes her late husband dec'd.

p.40 Dif betw Jane Riglesworth and Richd Sternell,re mending a boat, dismissed.

p.40 Attachmt to Peter Sexton for 1522 lb tobo agst the est of Thos Marsh. Francis Emperor is atty for Marsh who is now out of the Colony.

p.40 Certificate for 100 acres to Thos Browne for transporting himself and Anne his wife into this Colony.

p.40 Certif for 50 acres to Simond Peeters for transporting Alice Springwell into this Colony.

p.40 Certificate for 50 acres to Richd Hargrave for transporting one person, name not shown, into this Colony.

p.40 Major Tho Lambert ordered to pay Richd Chapman as atty for Barbara Hobson, widow, 4043 lb tobo, unless Lambert make it appear at next Court by oath of Savill Gaskin that Chapman refused to accept the tobo, then interest to be abated.

p.41 Goods bought by Simon Overzee mercht of Robte Attkinson mercht and delivered in Court upon oath and ordered recorded 16 Feb 1652/3.

Eleaven Anchors of Drams at 115 lb of tob the anchor	1317
Nyne peces of fustian at 70: per peece	0630
	- - -
	1947

p.41 Deposition of William Eale "aged about 32: yeres", sworn before the Governor and Council of Maryland 23 Dec 1652. That abt June 1651, being at the house of Coll Francis Yardley at Lynhaven in Virginia about some work, by appointment of Mr Jno Lownes, this deponent's master, this deponent was to do bricklaying and plastering there and at Kequotan, that he was taken off the work yet unfinished by his master.
Sworn before:
Will: Stone
Tho: Hatton
Job: Chandler

1652/3

p.41   A second deposition by Wm Eale sworn before the Governor and Council of Maryland, 23 Dec 1652.
That by an indenture here produced, subscribed by Mr Jno Lownes, dated
1st Dec 1647, he served Mr Lownes 4 years in the Barbadoes and Virginia,
from his arrival in the Barbadoes 3 March 1647/8 till the 3rd of March
last and about a week longer. He further swears that Mr Lownes, before
he came with him to Virginia promised to abate him 1/4th of a year in
consideration of his coming from the Barbadoes to Va.
Sworn before:
Will Stone
Tho: Hatton
Job: Chandler

p.41   Recorded 16 Feb 1652/3.   Jury in dif betw Mr Jno Lownes pltf and
Col Francis Yardley deft. They finding for the deft and the pltf to be
dismissed with costs of the suit.

Tho: Ivey	Richard Chapman
Richd Whitehurst	Tho: Ward
William Robinson	Gregory Parrett
John Godfrey	Richard Joanes
Edward Cannon	John Holmes
George Heigham	Robt Bowers

- The Jury above report that according to agreement the matter to be
decided betw Lt Col Cornelius Loyd and Mr Tho. Marsh.
- Also: The above Jury in dif betw John Rabley pltf and Tho Willoughby
Junior, deft, find, according to Court Order 15 Feb 1650/1, Willoughby
to pay 2747 lb tobo with interest.

1653

p.41   A Court held 15 April 1653.
      Present: Coll: William Clayborne Concill
          Coll: Francis Yardley   Mr Francis Emperor
          Leift: Coll: Cornelius Loyd Mr Thomas Bridge
          Mr Henery Woodhouse   Mr Thomas Goodrich
          Mr Lemuell Mason   Com'rs

p.41   Joane Yates, widow, appeared and demanded the thirds of land of
her late husband. She to have them "together with the Chiefe man'con
house thereuppon" for life.

p.41   Joane Yates, widow, to bring in inventory of her late husband's
estate.
His name does not appear in either of above entries. Perhaps later when
the inventory is recorded.

p.41 Dif betw Joane Yates widow, pltf, and Richd Yates, deft, referred
to next Court.

p.42   Dif betw Jno Holmes as assignee of Tho Woodwero pltf vs Henery
Snayle deft, referred to next Court.

p.42   That John Newman and Thos Leech in their lifetimes were joint
partners of an estate in this County. Tho Leech dying, upon an inquisition
it appeared that Newman had murdered him, for which he suffered death, as
may appear by record at James Citty. Order that the estate be sold at an
outcry the 4th of May next. That Mr. Henery Woodhouse be there to take
bills payable the next crop, and give account to the Court.

p.42   Geō Heigham, arrested by the Sheriff by a warrent from Jamestowne
at the suit of Carborough Kigan (or Rigan ?) to appear at June Court.
Tho Sayer engages himself to Wm Daynes now the Sheriff, in the sum of
5000 lb tobo for appearance of Heigham.

p.42   Probate of will of Robt Fowler to Mary Fowler his widow, she being
sole oxtrx.

p.42   Tho Wethell discharges Col Fr. Yardley from debt of 160 lb tobo
due to Abraham Sheeres the elder.

p.42 Jno Manning and Peter Sexton bound to good behavior for threatening
Francis Emperor gent with loss of life.
On submission of Jno Manning to this Court and to Emperor, he is released
from foregoing obligation.
Tho Lowne goes security for Peter Sexton.   (3 entries)

p.42   Jno Lowmes gent ordered to pay Wm Jermy 198 lb tobo Clerk's fees.

p.42   Dif betw Geo Heigham pltf and Capt Tho Burbage deft to next Court.

p.42   Dif betw Richd Conquest gent pltf vs Eliz Sibsey widow and extrx
of Capt Jno Sibsey in regard to division of the estate, appealed by Mrs
Sibsey to the Genl Court. Laurence Phillipps goes her security.

p.42   Richd Conquest, gent, petitions the Court that Elizabeth Sibsey,
widow, deliver a negro man servant to him "called by the name of black

Jacke" which of right belongs to his wife "she beinge sole heire unto
Thomas Sibsey deceased, late brother to the said Conquest his wife". Mrs
Sibsey ordered to deliver the servant.

Note: We do not quite understand this entry. See will of John Sibsey
on page 23 of these Abstracts. No mention of a son named Thomas who
would have been a brother of his dau Mary who married Rd Conquest. But
prob there was such a person unless the original record is in error.
It would therefore be assumed that the Mrs. Elizabeth Sibsey of these
records was not the mother of Thomas and Mary, but a later wife. B.F.

p.42   "Whereas Capt John Sibsey, about August last past made his last
will and testam't and therein bequeathed unto Mary Sibsey his sole
daughter" a servant a servant named John Payne (or Panne ?).
"Upon the peticon of Richard Conquest gent, who int'married with the
said Mary Sibsey", declaring to this Court that Elizabeth Sibsey, widow
and extrx of Capt Jno Sibsey, refuses to deliver the servant, etc. Mrs
Sibsey is ordered to deliver the servant to Conquest "for the use and
benefitt of his said wife . . . as in the said will is Expressed". Richd
Conquest to give security to Major Tho Lambert and Wm Jermy, Supervisors
of the will.

p.42   At a Court held 17 Jan last past, an attachmt was granted to Wm
Daynes, gent, Atty of Jno Jasperson, agst 2250 lb tobo of the estate of
Wm Westerhouse in the hands of Tho. Daynes, gent, Westerhouse being out
of the County. Westerhouse later notified by the Sheriff and not appearing, Judgt to pass agst the estate.

p.43   Mary Wickstead, widow, petitions that Capt Jno Sibsey, in last
August, in his will, bequeathed a cow called "goulden Locks" to her
daughter Elizabeth Wickstead. That Elizabeth Sibsey, extrx, refuses to
deliver the cow for the child's use.
Mrs. Sibsey is ordered to deliver the cow.

Note: This old sister does not appear from these records to be over
anxious to give up anything to anybody, regardless of who it belongs to.
                                                                B.F.

p.43   That Tho Allen, who is out of the Colony, owes Andrewe Warner
330 lb tobo. Order that Edwd Cannon, Allen's partner, make payment.

p.43   Edwd Cannon ordered to pay Andrewe Warner a debt of a man servant
with 4 years to serve, and also "One sufficient suite of cloathes for the
said Warner his wife". Both due by bill.

p.43   At a Court held 18 June 1650, a Judgt passed agst Capt John Sibsey
for payment of 4 servants to Mrs Anne Phillipps, widow, admrx of Mathewe
Phillipps, dec'd. Sibsey being security for Thomas Stegge, Junior, agent
for Capt Thomas Stegge, Esqr, Senior, from whom the servants were due.
The servants not yet paid, and Sibsey dead, his extrx is ordered to pay.

p.43   Richd Conquest, gent, ordered to pay Wm Jermy 500 lb tobo due for
fees from "the Wrecke of Capt: Lucke his Shipp" in Conquest's hands.

p.43   Attachmt to Coll Wm Clayborne for 900 lb tobo agst the estate of
Bartholomew Rench.
Also: Agst the est of Richd Hill for L 6. 7. 0 Sterling.
Also: Agst the est of Tobias Mathewes for 900 lb tobo "due for two yeres
      service with tenn yeres forbearance".

p.43   Attachmt to Lt Col Cornelius Loyd admr of Tho Tooker decd, for
2500 lb tobo agst the estate belonging to Capt: Luck's ship, it being a
wreck, in the hands of Richd Conquest.

p.43   Certificate for 200 acres to Edmund Bowman for transportation of
                himself   Richard Knight
              Thomas Scarbrooke   Edward Powell

p.43   Certificate for 300 acres to Laurence Phillipps for transporting
                Anne Finch   John Miller
                Mary Stanton   William Stevens
                John Cause   Richard Harlowe
"The two first are assigned over in Court to Robte Moodye" (Woodye ?)

p.43   Certificate for 100 acres to Lewes Farniall for transporting
              Allexander Forman   Elizabeth Price

p.43   Certificate for 250 acres to Tho Smith for transporting
                Elizabeth Kewer (Rower ?)
                Thomas Smith
                Sarah Smith
                Jane Smith
                Elizabeth Smith

p.43   Certif for 300 acres to Lt Col Cornelius Loyd for transporting
Will the Souldier, Thomas Lewes, Lewis Morgan, Two Scotchmen and Susan
a maide servant. All assigned over to Bartholomew Hoskins.

p.44   Certificate for 50 acres to Robte Woody for transporting himself.

p.44   Certificate for 800 acres to Tho Willoughby Junior for transporting:

Mary Bennett	John Muckeallen
Allexander Bell	William Fell
John Bell	Paul Trigge
John Gore	Grace Trigge
Joseph Toogood	John Savvidge
Peter Banden	Daniel Snoddy
James Wickard	Mathewe Hancocke
Richard Draper	George Hill

p.44   Certificate for 100 acres to John Rigge for transporting:
        Mary Shurlocke
        John Rigge Junr   (This name may be Kigge ?)

p.44   Certificate for 650 acres to Elizabeth Sibsey, widow, for transporting

Mary Evens	Allexander MackAllestre
Barbara Carter	Andrewe Nelson (Wolsen ?)
Anne Blacke	John Greene
James Milicent	John Peate (Prate ?)
David Southerley	Arthur Watson
Thomas Shrewe	William Hall

                    Thomas Dunton
All rights above assigned over to Jasper Hodgkinson.

Note: These names in themselves, their origin and their later variations
are interesting to some of us. How would you like to be named Toogood or
Snoddy ? Then my own ancestors Hodgskins. Later Hoskins. Hodgeskin is
actually Hog's skin, or what our modern pocket books and baggage is made
of - pigskin. Not that our ancestors had that kind of a hide, but they
made caps, jerkins, trousers out of that material. We presume such
clothing would last a lifetime. But again, how would you like to be
named the Son of a Hog's Skin ? Sterlingly honest, BUT -   B.F.

p.44   Constables chosen for 1653.

Nathaniel Carter from Daniell Tanners Creeke to Capt Willoughbeys
William Wilson for theEastern Branch in Elizabeth River
Marmaduke Marrington for the Southern branch of the same (this name does
     not appear to be Warrington as one would presume it to be. B.F.)
Thomas Greene for the Westerne branch thereof
Thomas Ward for the Little Creeke

(continued)

Constables chosen for 1653 (continued)

George Hawkins for the westerne Shoare in Lynhaven
Edward Cannon for the Easterne Shoare in Lynhaven.

Note: If Edward Cannon was so damned bad, then why was he selected to
enforce the Law ? Another example of the childlike quality of the 17th
century mind.   B.F.

p.44   The next Court to be held 16th May at the house of Savill Gaskin
in Lynhaven.

p.44   Owen Hayes registers mark for cattle and hogs. 15 April 1653.
Also: Francis Emperor, gent.   "
       Richard Whitehurst   "
       Richard Nicholls   "
       Edward Holmes   "   (5 entries)

p.44   An account of Peter Kinge debtor to Col Fr: Yardley recorded.

p.44   Recorded 15 April 1653. Thomas Horne of Elizabeth River, cooper,
gives "Jane Rigleworth (whom with the grace of God) I doe intend to
make my wedded wife" 2 cows now in her possession. Dated 16 March 1652/3.
Wit: John Finch   Signed   Thomas x Horne

p.45   Recorded 15 April 1653. Walter Grimes assigns land to Jno Piper
and Robte Bowers. Detail not shown, but see following entries. Dated 16
December 1648.
Wit: Geo White   Signed   Walter x Grimes
      Edmond Windett

Robte Bowers assigns over his share, being half of above land to Peter
Riglesworth. Dated 10 Dec 1649.
Wit: John Hill   Signed   Robte x Bowers
      Tho: Browne
Memo: The Bill of Sale made by Cornelius Loyd, gent, to the abovesaid
Walter Grimes, Robte Bowers, etc., was recorded 15 July 1648.
See next entry.

p.45   Recorded 15 April 1653.
Jane Riglesworth, widow of Peter Riglesworth late of Elizabeth River in
Co of Lower Norfolk, sends Greeting, etc. That Sir John Harvey, knt, Gov.
etc., gave a patent, dated 30 Nov 1638 to Cornelius Loyd for 400 acres
lying about 10 miles up the Western branch of the Elizabeth River on the

South side of the River, etc. That Loyd, for 5000 lb tobo pd by John
Piper, Robt Bowers and Walter Grimes of Elizabeth River, sold the 400
acres to them. That Grimes assigned his right to Piper and Bowers on 16
Nov 1648. That Bowers assigned his right to Peter Riglesworth late dec'd
husband of said Jane on 10 Dec 1649. Further that "John Piper the owner
of the other halfe of the said Land as is above specified Dyengeintestate,
Abigall the widdowe (and) relict of the said Piper did assign all her
right . . . towards the payment of the debts of the said Piper unto Peter
Riglesworth" on 10th of April 1651. That Peter Riglesworth covented to
sell to Robte Capps and Robert Springe, late of Nansimund, planters, 200
of the 400 acres. This 200 acres commonly called Pipers Land. The agreement being dated 8 July 1651, is now confirmed by Jane Riglesworth. This
entry dated 31 January 1652/3.
Wit: Signed   Jane x Riglesworth
John Finch
John Hill

p.46
     A Court held 16th May 1653
     Present
          Coll Francis Yardley   Mr Francis Emperor
          Mr John Sidney   Mr Thomas Bridge
          Mr Lemuell Mason   Com'rs

p.46 Mr Jno Hill and Mr Edmond Bowman to take inventory of estate of
Tho Tooker.

p.46   In dif betw Leift Coll Cornelius Loyd, atty of Richd Owens and
John Lownes, concerning a maid servant named Mary Gouldsmith. The Sheriff
to seize the maid and deliver her with her possessions to Loyd.

p.46   In dif betw Mary Fowler, widow, extrx of Robt Fowler, dec'd, and
Henery Snayle, concerning 350 acres at the head of the Southern branch of
the Little Creek, and assigned over by X'pofer Reynolds to the sd Fowler
in his lifetime. The Court orders that Henery Westgate, Giles Collins,
Thomas Workeman and Henery Brakes, lay out the 350 acres according to
agreement betw Snayle and Reynolds dated 18 Feb 1642 (? - this date
blotted and impossible to read). That Mr Francis Emperor be present. Mrs
Fowler and Snayle agree to abide their decision.

p.46   Dif betw Lumell Mason, gent, Attorney of Henery Sewell, vs Coll:
Francis Yardley, referred to next Court.

p.46   Simond Cornix fined 500 lb tobc for getting his woman servant
with child;
Note: This sort of thing just had to happen. These women, many culled
from the lowest walks of life in England and sold as servants in this
new country. Then placed alone with their masters (no other women any-
where about) on remote country places. What would you expect to have
happen ?   B.F.

p.46   That Col Fr Yardley obtained an attachmt agst the estate of Edwt
Standley in the hands of John Martin for 875 lb tobo. Martin as atty for
Standley discounts the a/c to 712 lb toboj etct

p.46   John Martin, Atty of Edwd Standley renounces his attorneyship.

p.46   Nathaniel Hayes ordered to pay Col Fr Yardley 100 lb tobo from
the estate he is possessed of, of Jno Spencer lately deceased.

p.46   Certificate for 100 acres to Giles Collins for transportation of
Nathaniell Wilson and John Everitt.

p.46   Certificate for 250 acres to Robte Powes for transportation of
                Robte Powes Senr   Mary Tudman
                John Powes   James Miller
                        William Griffin

p.46   Certificate for 100 acres to John Custis for Transporting Davy
Tompson and George Such.

p.46   Certificate for 50 acres to Jno Godfrey for transportation of a
maid servant assigned over to him by John Holmes.

p.46   Certificate for 650 acres to Simond Cornix for transporting
                Jane Cornix   William Patience
                Martha Cornix   George Lawson
                William Cornix   Plummer Bray
                Thomas Cornix   John Jennings
                Jane Simons   John Sealey
                Thomas Gregory   John Turner
                        John Brooke

Note: It was high time they came. We can only hope that now Simond was
fully satisfied. (see above)   B.F.

p.46   Next Court to be held 15th June at the house of Laurence Phillipps

p.47   Recorded 16 May 1653.   John Spencer mortgages household stuff
to Nicholas Mason to secure debt of 740 lb tobo. Dated 10 May 1653.
Wit: Signed   John Spencer
Samuell Coleman
Henery Westgate

p.47   Recorded 16 May 1653.
Will of Robte Fowler. Dated 23 Feb 1652/3.
To son Robte Fowler, at age of 21, 200 acres, part of land bought of Mr
     Christopher Reynolds, "and my beloved wife Mary Fowler, his mother,
     his guardian dueringe his minority"
To "my lovinge kinsman George Fowler my best wearinge suite of apparrell,
     with my best hatt, and my bible".
To wife Mary residue of estate, she extrx.
Wit: Thomas Bridge   Signed   Robert Fowler

p.47   Recorded 16 May 1653. Power of Atty. Dated 9th - (torn away)
1652. Robt Thomas of Elizabeth River to "my lovinge frend" Christopher
Rivers. To transact business.
Wit: Signed   Robert x Thomas
Edmond Bowman
Anthony x Farins

p.47.   Deed of Gift. Dated 20 April 1653. Richard Conquest of Elizabeth
River Parish, of Co of Lower Norfolk, gent., gives a negro man servant
named Black Jack to his wife Mary. She formerly Mary Sibsey, daughter of
Capt John Sibsey, dec'd. Also "as sole heir unto her brother Thomas
Sibsey longe since deceased". He also gives 3 cows, a feather bed, etc.,
given by Capt John Sibsey to them shortly after their marriage, etc.
Wit: Signed   Ri: Conquest
Lemuell Mason
Anne Mason
Daniell Tanner
Wm Hattersley
Acknowledged in Court and recorded 16 May 1653.

p.48   Deed. Dated 1 May 1653. Acknowledged and recorded 16 May 1653.
Henery Snayle of the Little Creek in the parish of Lynhaven, sells
Henery Westgate of the same place, planter, 110 acres of land formerly
assigned to him (Snayle) by Robte Hayes late of Little Creek. Land
begins at a marked tree by the Bever Damms, to a tree in Oken Swamp, etc.
Wit: Lemuell Mason.   Signed   Henr: x Snayle
     Will Jermy

p.48   Power of Atty. 4 May 1652. John Rice of the Citty of London,
Chirurgeon, to Leift: Thomas Keelinge of Lynhaven in Va. to transact
business.   Signed   John Rice
Wit: Ed: Hall, Chirurgeon
                        Recorded 8 June 1653.

p.48   A Court held 15th June 1653.
        Present
            Leift Coll Cornelius Loyd   Mr Thomas Bridge
            Major Thomas Lambert   Mr Thomas Goodrich
            Leift: Coll: John Sidney   Mr Lemuell Mason   Com'rs

p.48   Certificate for 200 acres to George Kempe for importing
            Dorothy Wincoth   John Blunt
            Peter Joyce   Nathaniel Gibbs

p.48   Certificate for 200 acres to Wm Robinson for importing
            Wm Robinson Senr   Susanna Robinson
            Wm Robinson Junr   Daniell Makey
Memo: Robinson assigns above rights to George Kempe.

p.48   Dif betw Eliz Sibsey, widow, pltf and Tho Ivey deft to next Court.

p.49   James Smith ordered to pay 75 lb tobo due, with forbearance, to
Richd Sternell.

p.49   Dif betw Richd Pinner Atty of Henery Robinson, pltf, and William
Jermy Atty of Major Tho Lambert, deft, referred to "untill the arrivall
of the next Shipping out of England into this Country".

p.49   In case of several actions entered by Christopher Rivers agst
Jno Lownes gent, attachmt agst the est of Lownes for 1500 lb tobo.

p.49   Jno Lownes gent to deliver upon oath all est he has of Captain
Mathewe Woods dec'd to Tho Goodrich gent, Admr of Woods, etc.

p.49   Henery Hinson ordered to pay Nathaniell Carter 300 lb tobo due him.

p.49   That John Lownes gent obtained and order agst Col Fr: Yardley at

last Quarter Court at James City, for certain tobo. That Col Claybourne,
Secretary, being present at this Court, and showing cause, an attachmt
is granted Yardley agst the said tobo, etc. This entry is not clear.

p.49   Gregory Parrett, who married the relict of Tho Tooker dec'd, to
give security to disengage Lt Col Cornelius Loyd, Admr of Tooker's est.
Then Parrett to take admr in his hands, or otherwise to deliver all the
est to Loyd "as well that was given by Hatton his will unto the late
relicte of the said Tooker and now the wife of the said Parrett as otherwise. And that therebe a devision made of the said Hattons Estate
according to will, betweene her and the Children of the said Hatton".

p.49   Dif betw Richd Sternell, pltf, vs Tho Godby, deft, concerning
land in the Western Branch of Elizabeth River parish, ref to next Court
to be fully determined. They to bring patents, etc.

p.49   Major Cornelius Loyd admr of Tho Tooker ordered to pay Major Tho
Lambert 1307 lb tobo.

p.49   Cases finished and determined:
Thos Bridge vs Richd Conquest, gent.
Jno Sidney, gent, vs Edwin Wilder
Tho Daynes, gent, vs Tho Everage
Tho Edmonds vs Geo Heigham
Jno Sidney, Atty of Francis Wells, vs Tho Dadford
Mathew Fassett vs John Porter
Lemuell Mason, gent, Atty of Henery Sewell, vs Francis Yardley, gent.
(The above entry, names, etc., being in Latin is therefore open to
question in detail. B.F.)

p.50   Deed of Lease. 24 April 1651. Cornelius Loyd "livinge by Elizabeth
River in the County of Lower Norffolke in the Country of Virginia gent:
assignee of Edward Loyd his brother, who is guardian unto Samuell Hawkins
an Orphan", leases to Thomas Ward of the Little Creek of the Co of Lower
Norfolk, planter, a tract of land, acerage not shown, known " by the name
of Woolves Necke lyinge neere the Little Creeke" until the said Samuell
Hawkins be 21 years of age. The property includes "one tennebable dwell-
inge house Thirty foote of length". Ward to plant an orchard, etc.
Wit: Signed   Cornelius Loyd
Henery Coursey
Richard Pinner
Will: Jermy

p.50   Ordered to be Recorded 15 August 1653.
Deed of Gift. 4 March 1652/3. Thos Lambert, gent, gives "unto my Kins-
man George Glane the younger" a heifer bred of a cow lately sold by said
Lambert to George Glane the elder. The heifer now at Lambert's plantation
called Puggetts Necke.
Wit: Signed   Thomas Lambert
Tho: Bridge
Will: Jermy

p.51   Recorded 15 Aug 1653.
Deed of Gift. 3 March 1652/3. Tho Lambert gives George Glane a cow.
Wit: Signed   Tho: Lambert
Walter Huckstep
Tho: Bridge

p.51   At a Court held 15th August 1653.
        Present
            Coll: Francis Yardley   Mr William Mosley   (sic)
            Leift: Coll: Cornelius Loyd Mr Thomas Bridge
            Leift: Coll: John Sidney   Mr Thomas Goodrich
            Mr Lemuell Mason   Com'rs

p.51   Dif betw Capt Thomas Willoughbye pltf and Emanuell Delrcowe deft
referred to next Court.
Note: This name open to question. Possibly a corruption of Delarue, which
was later a well known name in Virginia.   B.F.

p.51   The following, each seperate entries in the original record, are
referred to the next Court.
Capt Tho Willoughbye pltf vs Mary the wife of Wm Hattersley deft.
William Johnson pltf vs Simond Cornix
Christopher Rivers pltf vs Jno Lownes, gent, deft.
Tho Daynes pltf vs Tho Everage deft.
Jno Sidney, gent, Attorney of Fr: Wells, pltf vs Tho Dadford, deft.
Lemuell Mason, gent, Attorney of Henery Sewell, pltf, vs Coll: Fr.Yardley

p51   Jno Chandler ordered to pay Nicholas Freeman 620 lb tobo at next
crop.

p.51   Tho Sayer, late guardian to Robte Fitts who is now of age, ordered
to deliver him his estate.

1653

p.51   John Porter, who intermarried with the administratrix of John Cooke, decd, ordered to pay Mathewe Fassett, marriner, 250 lb tobo due from the estate.

p.51   Eliz: Sibsey, widow and extrx of Jno Sibsey decd, ordered to pay 1000 lb tobo due to John Robins, administrator of Wm Moore, decd.

p.51   Jno Lownes, gent, in dif betw him and Lt Col Cornelius Loyd, Atty of Wm Eaton, appeals to the Genl Court at James Citty.

p.51   In dif Tho Bridge, gent, pltf, vs Richd Conquest, gent, deft, Conquest appeals to the Genl Court at James City.

p.52   Edward Holmes nonsuited in action agst Edw: Parker for nonappearance

p.52   Certificate for 250 acres to George Glane for transporting
                Himself and Mary his wife   Anthony Clarke
                George Glane the younger   Anne Maston

p.52   Certificate for 50 acres to Wm Johnson for transporting Frances Thompson.

p.52   Certificate for 100 acres to Mary Burrowes for transporting
                John Townsend   Elizabeth Chuckett

p.52   Lists of tytheable persons to be taken by the following:
Thomas Dadford for the Eastern branch in Elizabeth River
Francis Fleetwood for the Southern branch there
Richard Pinner for the Western branch there
Laurence Phillipps from Daniell Tanners Creek to Capt: Willoughbyes
John Holmes for the Little Creek
Edward Cannon for the Easterne shoare in Lynhaven
John Martin for the Westerne shoare there

p.52   Upon special occasions a Court to be held at the house of William Johnson in Lynhaven on next Monday, the 22 July, concerning the cargo of the ship called the White Swan "beinge lately taken as Prize".

p.52   Ordered to be recorded this 15th of August 1653.
Richard Sternell aged thirty eight yeres or there abouts sworne and

Ex'mied saith that about the Sixth of June last past, he this Depon't beinge on board the Shipp called the Loepoldus, shee the said Shipp beinge at anchor in Elizabeth River in the County of Lower Norffolk in Virginia did see mr Gunnell and mr Reade masters of London Shipps, their shipps beinge att anchor in James River in the part called Newports Newes, which said two masters came on board the said Leopoldus with a wherry and fower or five men with them which he this depon't supposed to be their owne Seamen.

That Read and Gunnell demanded from whence the ship came and were told by the officers from Dunkurke. The London Masters demanded the commission from the officers and were told it had been carried by their Captain to the Governor. Then some discussion in which the London masters said they had power to command Leift: Coll: Cornelius Loyd to assist them, he then being on board. There was considerable argument, the London masters demanded to examine the ship, and finally left a man on board to secure them. "and the said Officers of the said Shipp said that if they left a man on board uppon force, that they would throwe him the said man over board and did proffer to throwe him over, but had mercy upon the said man, and tooke him and carried him on shoare immediately, Gunnell and Read being then in sight and see what was done".

                                        Signed   Richard Sternell
Sworn in Court 15 August 1653.

p.52   "Robert Wooddy aged about Two and thirty yeeres", sworn, says about as above. After the dispute with Gunnell and Read "the Skipper said to Coll: Clayborne and others who then came aboard if they were Prize to the Country. And if they pleased to send fifty men they should be welcome"
                                        Signed   Robte Wooddy
Sworn in Court 15 August 1653

p.53   Inventory of the Estate of Capt John Sibsey, dec'd, taken 3rd Sept 1652 by Lemuell Mason, Wm Jermy, Tho Ivey and George Kempe. This is a very long inventory containing a list of individual silver items, etc., etc. Totals 68313 lb tobo. Covers pages 53-54-55. Sworn 15 August 1653 by Elizabeth Sibsey.

p.55   Inventory of the Estate of Christopher Burrowes, gent, taken 4th Feb 1652/3 by Tho Bridge, Edward Hall, Tho. Keeling and Will Robinson. Totals 35477 lb tobo. Includes:

John Townsend about one yere to serve	0600 lb tobo
Elizabeth Chukett haveing about one yere to serve	0300
Henery Halsey having fower yeres to serve	2800
George Vallentine havinge three yeres to serve	1600
William Anthony haveinge five yeres to serve	2000
An Indian havinge tenn yeres to serve	2200

(This is an interesting 17th century inventory)

p.56   Patent. 2 March 1647/8. Sir Wm Berkeley to Tho Godby, 200 acres
in Lower Norfolk, on N side of a branch of the W branch of Elizabeth
River called the Clarks Creeke, for importing 4 persons, names not shown.
                                   Signed   William Berkeley
The above patent assigned by Tho Godby to Robt Loneday. 9 Dec 1648.
Wit: Thos Tooker   Signed   Tho x Godby

p.57   Recorded 17 Aug 1653.
Deed. 10 Oct 1652. Edwd Hall, Chirurgeon, of Lynhaven parish, sells
Savill Gaskin of Lynhaven, planter, a tract of land (acreage not shown)
known as Scull Necke.
Wit: Richard x Gardner   Signed   Edward Hall Chirurg'

p.57   Power of Atty. 6 March 1647/8. Recorded 17 Aug 1653. Jno Dawber
"by Gods grace intendinge to goe for Wngland" to Wm Daynes to transact
business. This name may possibly be Damber.
Wit: Thomas x Buckmaster   Signed   John Dawber

p.58   A Court held 15 Oct 1653
       Present
            Mr Henery Woodhouse   Mr Lemuell Mason
            Major Thomas Lambert   Mr Thomas Bridge   Com'rs

p.58   In dif betw Jno Sidney, gent, Atty of Francis Wells, vs Thomas
Dadford, Sidney is nonsuited for not appearing.

p.58   Col Francis Yardley ordered to answer complaint made agst him by
Edwd Robinson.

p.58   Dif betw John Holmes, assignee of Thos Woodward, pltf, and Henery
Snayle, deft, referred to next Court.

p.58   Order the John Stratton senior bring in inventory of the estate
of Thomas Stratton his late son deceased, to be recorded for benefit of
"Robte Stratton brother and right heire of the said Thomas Stratton".

p.58   Edmund Bowman, merchant, is nonsuited in action against John
Godfrey for unjust molestation.

p.58   That at a Court held 17 January last past Edw Cannon was fined
600 lb tobo, 300 lb of which was remitted. Cannon now petitions that the
balance be remitted "In regard of his present poverty". This granted.

p.58   Arthur Egleston to be paid 300 lb tobo from the estate of John
Newman for "greate paines and trouble he had in and about the takinge
upp and burienge of the Corpes of Thomas Leech deceased who was murdered
by John Newman".

p.58   An order from the Governor, dated James Citty, 8 July 1653, that
half of the estate of John Newman and Tho Leech be delivered to William
Jermy, Atterney of John Mendham for his use. The other half to the County.

p.58   That in a Court order 16th May last, Gyles Collins, Thomas
Workeman, Henery Brakes and Henery Westgate were to lay out a tract of
land in dif betw Henery Snayle and Mary Fowler widow and relict of Robt
Fowler. It appearing to the Court "the said Westgate not to be a com-
petent man in the said matter", that upon petition of Nicholas Mason
who intermarried with the said Mary Fowler, order that Lancaster Lovett
be appointed in place of Westgate.

p.58   Court to be adj to 1st Nov next. Wm Jermy, Clerk, etc.

p.59   Recorded 15 Oct 1653. Order to the Commissioners of Lower Norfolk
County to deliver half of the estate of John Newman and Tho Leech to John
Mendham. Dated James Citty, 8 July 1653. Signed Ri: Bennett
(see above)

p.59   Recorded 15 Oct 1653. Power of Atty. John Mendham "in the County
of James Towne in Virginia planter", admr of Tho Leech, late of the County
of Lower Norfolk, deceased, to "my beloved frend" Wm Jermy of Lower
Norfolk, gent, to settle the estate of Leech. Dated 19 March 1652/3.
Wit: Tho: Fulcher   Signed   John Mendham

p.59   A list of cattle of the estate of Jno Newman and Tho Leech sold
at outcry by Mr Henery Woodhouse.   lb tobo
Imprimis   one ould Cowe call'd Tinker and steere calve to
     Michaell Clarke for   470
Itm one Cowe called Blackbird sould to Henery Needham   470
Itm one Cowe called Budgett and cowe calve to Griffin Given   590
Itm one heifer called Trull to mr Norwood   380
Itm one Cowe called Penny and calve and a Little Bull to
     Robte Davis

(continued next page)

The Estate of Newman and Leech - continued.

		lb tobo
Itm	One Cowe called Mopns and bull to George Bisley	510
Itm	Three Hoggs sould to mr Hall at	350
Itm	One ould Gunne sould to Robte Davis	070
		- - -
	Sum: total	3390

p.59   A Court held 1st Nov 1653
        Present
            Leift: Coll: Cornelius Loyd   Mr William Moseley
            Major Thomas: Lambert   Mr Francis Emperor
            Leift: Coll: John: Sidney   Mr Thomas Bridge
            Mr: Lemuell: Mason   Mr Thomas Goodwin   Com'rs

p.59   Dif betw Capt Tho Willoughby, pltf, and Manuell Dolweere to next
Court. This name also appears as Emanuell in the entry.

p.59   In dif betw Capt Tho Willoughby pltf and Andrewe Nicholls deft,
Nicholls ordered to acknowledge he wronged Willoughby and to pay Court
charges.

p.59   Capt Tho Willoughby makes it appear he had an agreement with
Michael Laurence to break six steers for 400 lb tobo, an axe and a hoe.
Laurence is ordered to keep his contract.

p.60   The Sheriff ordered to arrest Margrate Hattersley, wife of Wm
Hattersley, accused by Capt Tho Willoughby of felony, and produce her
at next Court.

p.60   Attachmt agst est of Wm Capps for 2510 lb tobo to Lt Col Cornelius
Loyd in behalf of Sir William Berkeley.

p.60   Dif betw Sir Wm Berkeley and Owen Hayes, deft, to next Court.

p.60   In dif betw Francis Emperor, gent, and Thomas Edmonds, concerning
a boat belonging to Mr Tho: Daynes, that was lost, Emperor to be fully
discharged and free from same.

p.60   A warrant to be issued agst George Heigham "for sufferinge
drunkenesse and disorderly company in his house uppon the Sabboth day".

p.60   Geo Heigham ordered to put in security for the appearance of his
wife Deborah who was arrested at the suit of John Sidney, gent, she
having failed to appear.

p.60   Dif betw Simond Peeters pltf and Henery Merritt to next Court.

p.60   "Whereas John Lownes hath in a most scandalous grosse and contemptuous manner under the hand writeinge of the said Lownes in most
opprobrious termes abused Leift: Coll: Cornelius Loyd by writinge these
words followinge vizt: I: (meaning the said Lownes) have beene often
before you (meaning the sd mr Loyd) and in stead of receivinge Justice
I have had abuses by you and your wife".
    Lownes being present and unable to prove this, is ordered to ask,
in open Court, Loyd's pardon, to acknowledge he has done Loyd "greate
wronge and that he is sorry for it". Lownes is further fined a hhd of
tobo for the use of the Country.

p.60   "Upon the humble peticon of John Lownes, as alsoe his open submission to this Court, and with the consent of Leift: Coll: Cornelius
Loyd, this Court hath thought meete to remitt thabovsd fine:".

Note: There is right much false alarm in these records. Observe the
terrifying words in the above entries. all of which amounted to nothing.
                                                                    B.F.

p.60   John Lownes ordered to pay 300 lb tobo for damages to Christopher
Rivers for several suits brought unjustly against him and his wife. Also
Lownes to pay 400 lb tobo Court charges.

p.60   Certificate for 450 acres to Lt. Col. Cornelius Loyd for importing
                William Hill   Tho Willows   (?)
                Thomas Morgan   Wm Parker
                Wm Bennett   John Godby
                Gyles Godfrey   Wm Dorsey
                        Hugh Williams
Mr. Loyd assigns all these rights in open Court to John Bowles

p.60   Dif betw John Dyer, pltf, vs Richard Avrill, deft, referred to
next Court.

p.61   Certificate for 650 acres to Major Tho Lambert for importing
                Patriarke White   Robert Bennett
                Richard Dixon   Robert Heedinge
                John a Moore   Thomas Cox
                Danll Dawills   Richard Orpdrood   (?)
                Elizabeth Wood   Roger - (surname omitted)
                Millicent Simons   George Bullocke
                            Samuell Coleman

p.61   Attachmt to Tho Davis for 200 lb tobo agst est of John Meares,
merchant, for service. The said Meares now out of this Colony.

p.61   Jno Godfrey to pay Edmund Bowman, merchant, 2300 lb tobo and 2
bbl corn due for a maid servant.

p.61   Dif betw Charles Rose, pltf,vs Geo Heigham,deft, to next Court.

p.61   Dif betw Wm Daynes and Thos Daynes pltfs vs Tho Edmonds to next
Court.

p.61   Tho Godby to pay James Smith 40 lb tobo for expense, in that Smith
arrested Anne the wife of Godby to this Court, but she failing to appear
no proceedings could be had against her.

p.61   John Sonsey registers his mark for cattle. (1st Nov. 1653)

p.61   The following cases referred to next Court.
Tho Edmonds vs Robt Grimes, deft.
Jno Holmes assignee of Tho Woodward vs Savill Gaskin
John Holmes vs James Thelaball, deft.
Coll: Yardley vs George Glane deft.
Lemuell Mason, gent, Atty of Henery Sewell vs Col. Fr: Yardley.

p.61   An Orphans Court to be held 14th Dec at the house of Laurence
Phillipps.

p.61   Recorded 1 Nov 1653.
Power of Atty. Dated 10 March 1650/1. Richard Ackton to "wellbeloved
frend" Richard Whitehurst of the Eastern branch in Elizabeth River in

Virginia, to collect debts and transact other business in Virginia.
Wit: Signed   Richard Ackton
Henery Woodhouse
William Moseley

Richard Whitehurst assigns, in behalf of Richd Acton, lands in a certain
bill of sale to Mathewe Mathias and Daniell Douglas. Dated 1 Nov 1653.
Wit: Signed   Richard Whitehurst
Fra: Emperor
Will: Jermy
Note: The bill of sale referred to was Recorded 15 Aprill 1648

p.62   In difference betw Mrs Elizabeth Sibsey, pltf, and Mr Thos Ivy,
deft, the Jury, for the vindication of her good name, agree "that the
said Ivy shall stand in open Court the next that shall be held in this
place from nine till 3 in the after noone with these exprest words in
Capitall letters standinge before and behind on his hatt, I (Tho Ivy)
doe confess and acknowledge to have wrongfully defamed Mrs: Elizabeth
Sibsey of the County of Lower Norffolk for which I am hartyly sorry and
Crave her pardon: And moerover to stand in the same manner at the Court
house doore in publique veiw at James Citty the next Grand Assembly the
second day after the Assembly sitts, from 9 in the morninge till 3 in the
afternoone and likewise to pay all costs and Chardges that hath been
spent in this suite"

                            The Jury
            Tho Daynes   Timothy Ives
            Tho Ward   John Bowsey
            Tho Smith   X'pofer Rivers
            Tho Dadford   Richard Whitehurst
            Tho Davys   Will Hattersley
            Tho Cartwright   Richard Sternell

Note:
We imagine that Mr. Ivy would have lost taste for his name Thomas after
that.   B.F.

Note No.2   It further occurs to me that when I become too old and dis-
agreeable to make Abstracts, that I will get myself up in costume of the
period, put such signs on my hat, and hire myself out to Williamsburg,
Inc., to stand at the door of the Assembly Room in the Capitol. The hours
are specified, the pay should be good and the work not too heavy for an
elderly gent. Please do not apply for this job before I can get there.
                                                                         B.F.

1653

p.62   "Those whose names are here underwritten beinge appoynted to Veiw
the Corps of Ann the wife to Savill Gaskin . . . That though it pleased
god shee dyed a sudden and unexpected death, yet no waise accysary to her
owne death, nor yet by the cause of any other suffered.
        Witnes our hands this 31th of October 1653"

John Ware	John Martin
Thos Davyes	Lancaster Lovet
Owin Hayes	Lawrence Plumer

p.62   Deed. 19 Oct 1653. Owen Morgin, seaman, sells for 1200 lb tobo,
to "my good frend John Dyer", a parcel of land betw Mr Tho Allen's
swamp and the swamp by the now dwelling house of sd Jno Dyer.
Wit: Signed   Owin Morgin
Thomas Hall
Edward Robinson

p.62   1st Nov 1653. Payments to be made from the County Levies.

	lb tobo
To the Publique	6135
To Leift: Coll Cornelius Loyd for Burgesses Chardges	1932
To Coll: Francis Yardley for his Burgesses Chardges	1000
To Leift Coll John Sidney for two persons wanting in his Levy last yere	0130
To mr Wm Daynes in consideracon of the Prison	0700
To Lauw: Phillipps in consideracon of troublinge his house	0600
To Major Lambert for two paire of Hinges	0100
To John Martin for his servant 14 dayes goeinge up with the Burgesses	0140
To mr Thomas Goodrich for his boate hire 19: dayes with the Burgesses	0190
To mr Lemuell Mason for a Woolfe, and a Levye last yere	0165
To Robte Powes	0230
To Mr William Jermy Clerke	0300
To Jasper Hoskins for goeinge with the Burgesses to towne 20 dayes	0300
To Fardinando Batty for Rowinge upp the Burgesses to towne	0140
To John Smith for waitinge on the Burgesses	0120
To Robte Yonge for waitinge on the Burgesses	0100
To Mr Lee for a barr in the Court house	1000
To Richard at Mrs Burroughes her house	0130
To Thomas Hall for killinge one Wolve	0100
To Wm Shapwell for waitinge on the Burgesses	0100
To George Merritt for the like	0120
To Simon Cornix for his servant and boat to attend the Burgesses	0220
	- - - -
fwd	13952

Fwd	13952
To mr William Moseley for 2 persons over rated Ao 1651	0076
To Robte Woody the Undershreive	0300
To mr Thomas Bridge Over Rated the last Yere	0065
To mr Richard Conquest for his man that Died in the Countyes service	0500
To the french man at Coll'o Yardleyes for his attendce of the Burg:	0150
To the fidler for his slieght attendance of the Burgesses	0150
To Richard Joanes for one person under age paid the last yeres Levy	0065
To mr John Piggott for his boate for the Counties use	0060
To Laurence Phillipps	0578
To Sallery at tenne per Cent	1531
	- - - -
Sum total	17427

p.63   To meet the foregoing, a levy of every taxable person in the County, according to the list given in, 471 persons at 37 lb tobo per poll.

p.63   Leift Coll Cornelius Loyd to collect for the Western branch in Elizabeth River from 101 persons and ordered to pay as follows

To sallery	0374
To himselfe by account	1932
To John Smith	0120
To Wm Shapwell	0100
To George Merritt	0120
To mr William Daynes	0700
To mr Goodrich	0190
To Richard Joanes	0065
To mr Piggott	0060
To Mr: Mosely	0076
	- - - -
	3737

p.63   Major Tho: Lambert to collect for the Eastern and Southern branches in Elizabeth River from 122 persons, and ordered to pay as follows:

To Sallery	0430
To Sack: Brewster	0522
To John Fripps	1000
To Laurence Phillipps	0600
To Mr Lee	1000
To Fardinando Batty	0140
To Robte Yonge	0100

(continued)

Major Lambert's List (continued).

	lb tobo
To Robte Woody	0300
To himselfe	0100
To Laurence Phillipps	0322
	- - - -
	4514

p. 63   Mr Francis Emperor to collect for the Western Shore in Lynhaven
from 78 persons and ordered to pay as follows:

To sallery	0228
To Coll Yardley	1000
To the fidler	0150
To the Frenchman at Coll Yardleys	0150
To Richard at mrs Burrowes	0130
To Robte Powes	0023
To Simon Cornix	0220
To John Martin	0140
To Laurence Phillipps	0578
	- - - =
	2886

p. 63   Leift: Coll: John Sidney to collect for the Eastern Shore in
Lynhaven parish from 59 persons and ordered to pay as follows

To sallery	0218
To himselfe	0130
To Thomas Hall	0100
To Mr Webster	1735
	- - - -
	2183

p. 64   Mr Tho: Bridge to collect for Little Creek from 71 persons and
ordered to pay as follows

To sallery	0262
To himselfe	0065
To Mr Richard Conquest	0500
To Mr Webster	1800
	- - = -
	2627

p. 64   Mr Lemuell Mason to collect from Daniell Tanners Creek to Capt
Willoughbyes from 40 persons and ordered to pay as follows

To sallery	148
To Mr Webster	465
To Jasper Hoskins	300
To Mr William Jermy	360
To himselfe	165
To Laurence Phillipps	102
	- - - -

p.64   A Court held at the house of Coll'o Francis Yardley 11 Nov 1653
       Present
            Coll: Francis Yardley   Mr Francis Emperor
            Leift: Coll: John Sidney   Mr Thomas Bridge   Com'rs

p.64   Certificate for 350 acres to John Taylor for importing
            Wm Savige   Robte Savige
            Anne Savige   Wm Kinge
            Fran: Savige   Joseph Dozewell
                    Mary a maide servant

p.64   Thos Cheeley being 65 years of age "and a Decreped man" to be
free from all taxes.

p.64   Recorded 15 Dec 1653. Power of Atty. Dated 12 Nov 1653. Francis
Yardley to "my welbeloved wife Mrs Sarah Yardley" and "my lovinge frend
Mr Simond Hancocke" to transact business.
Wit: Signed   Fran: Yardley
John Sidney
Francis Emperor

p.64   Recorded 15 Dec 1653. Receipt. Dated 6 Oct 1653. Sir William
Berkeley, kt, acknowledges to have received from Coll: Francis Yardley,
26 oxen for which he has paid "the same of One Hundred pounds sterling
in Goods at the first penny" in full satisfaction.
Wit: Signed   William Berkeley
Wm Hill   Fran: Yardley
Wm Whitbye

Note: I have not forgiven Sir William for the 14 original letters of
his that I read. He knew so much that we want to know. But he had the
fine art of saying nothing whatever in the written word. He wrote an
open round hand, easy to read, that is if you would care to read these
formal vacuums.   B.F.

p.64   Recorded 15 Dec 1653. "Nicholas Seaborne aged about thirty and
Nyne yeres sworn and Ex'aied this 15th day of December 1653
       Saith that in August last was Seaventeene Yeres since, this Depon't
left a boate at Mr Cages his house for the use of Leif't Barkelett this
Depon't beinge at that tyme servant to John Yates shippwright
                              the marke of
                              Nicholas x Seaborne"

Note: This would date the incident back to 1636. The 2nd letter in
Barkelett's name is actually illegible, being blotted out.   B.F.

p.65   Recorded 15 Dec 1653. Edward Booker of Rotterdam, merchant, discharges Thomas Allen of Lynhaven from all debts. Dated 12 Apl 1651.
Signed   Edward Booker

p.65   Will of Daniell Tanner. Dated 17 Nov 1653. Recorded 15 Dec 1653.
To Mr Lemuel Mason all estate on South side of James River and all debts
    due.
To Mrs Anne Mason "for her great paynes and care and love towards me"
    3600 lb tobo to be paid from estate in hands of Thos Sherley.
To Mrs Elizabeth Thelaball 600 lb tobo in hands of Tho: Sherley.
To John Worsnam a heifer.
To James Simonds the tobo he owes and 40 lb tobo due from Jasper
    Hoskinson.
To Tho: Sherley the residue of estate in Virginia for the use of his
    child "provided the Child be Christened and named Daniell".
Exor: Mr Lemuel Mason.
Overseers: Thomas Sherley and Florentyne Payne.
Wit: Signed   Daniell Tanner
Rich: Conquest
Robte Butler

p.65   A Court held 15 December 1653.
        Present
            Leift Coll Cornelius Loyd   Mr Wm Moseley
            Major Tho. Lambert   Mr Francis Emperor
            Leift: Coll: John Sidney   Mr Tho: Bridge
            Mr Lemuel Mason   Mr Tho: Goodrich   Com'rs.

p.65   In dif betw Charles Rose, pltf, and George Heigham, deft,
Heigham is ordered to pay Rose 487 lb tobo and 4 bbl corn.

p.65   Emanuel Dolveere ordered to pay Capt Tho Willoughby 1000 lb tobo.

p.65   Judgt to Wm Jermy on behalf of Sir Wm Berkeley, kt, and late Governor, agst Owen Hayes for 498 lb tobo due by bill.

p.65   In dif betw Col Fr: Yardley, pltf, and George Glane, deft, an
appeal is made by Glane to the General Court. Tho Lambert his security.

p.65   Attachmt for 350 lb tobo to Lemuel Mason as assignee of James
Thelaball agst the estate of Tho Morgan.

p.65   Probate of will of Danl Tanner to Lemuel Mason, gent.

p.65   Dif betw Lemuell Mason, gent, Atty for Henery Sewell vs Col. Fran:
Yardley referred to next Court.

p.66   Tho Edmonds ordered to acknowledge his fault in abusing William
Daynes and Thos Daynes gent.

p.66   Capt Tho Willoughby complains of loss of his cattle by others
using his mark. His mark confirmed and to remain unless Major Lambert
or others can justly claim the cattle.

p.66   In dif betw Robte Yeu assignee of Tho Morgan vs Thos Willoughby
Junior, gent, no order to pass agst Willoughby.

p.66   Tho Ward and Gyles Collins ordered to appraise the estate belonging to the orphans of John Lankefeild deod in the custody of Tho Workeman. The Goods to be sold and the proceeds laid out in cattle for the
orphans.

p.66   On reference to this Court by the Governor and Council, of a
cause betw Wm Whitbye, gent, pltf, vs Elizabeth Sibsey, widow, extrx of
Capt John Sibsey, deod, deft., Order that Eliz Sibsey return to Whitbye
the bill of Mrs Anne Phillipps for 2046 lb tobo and a note of Mr.
Phillipps for 1200 lb tobo, both due to Peeter Clauson whose attorney
Whitbye is.

p.66   Dif betw Jno Holmes pltf vs James Thelaball deft dismissed. No
cause for action.

p.66   Dif betw Col Fr: Yardley pltf vs Darby Kelly deft to next Court.

p.66   Richd Avrill ordered to pay Jno Dyer 480 lb tobo due him.

p.66   Edward Cannon ordered to pay Col Fr Yardley, assignee of Edward
Hall, chirurgeon, 470 lb tobo due him.

p.66   Tho Allen ordered to pay Peeter Ashton, gent, attorney of Edward
Booker, gent, 1200 lb tobo due him.

p.66   Prob of will of Wm Smith to Mary Smith his widow and sole extrx.

p.66   Dif betw Tho Allen, pltf, vs Geo Raymond, deft, dismissed. No cause for action. Allen to pay charges for unjust molestation.

p.66   Lemuel Mason, gent, guardian of Henery Sewell the orphan of Henery Sewell, deceased, ordered to pay Jno Sidney, gent, 340 lb tobo due him from the estate.

p.66   Anthony Sizeman ordered to pay Tho Workman, Attorney for Addam Hayes, 712 lb tobo due him.

p.66   In dif betw Tho Andrewes, pltf, and Tho Greene deft, Greene to pay damages for nonappearance.

p.67   On petition of Nicholas Mason, who married the relict of Robert Fowler, showing that Oct last it was ordered that Mr Emperor and four others lay out a certain tract of land in dif betw Henery Snayle and the widow and extrx of Fowler, which was done. Snayle is now ordered to make a firm bill of sale to Nicholas Mason for the use of Robert Fowler, son of the said Robt Fowler, deceased.

Note: There is a certain literary convention of the cruelty of step parents to the children of former marriages. I see no sign of this what-soever in these old Virginia records. Again and again I've come upon suits instituted by step-parents, and wills left by them, in which the children were always being protected and cared for by them. While of course there were such cases, I never happen to have seen any record of any thing that would indicate that the children were treated in any way but with regard and affection.   B.F.

p.67   Attachmt to Simond Overzee, mercht, for 3000 lb tobo due him from the estate of Roger Fountayne.

p.67   That Robt Davis sued Geo Raymond in this Court and then "surceased his said suit". On petition of Raymond, Davis is ordered to pay him 200 lb tobo damages "in regard he the said Raymond is Master of a Shipp and hath attended at this Court with greate Expence, and Charge".

p.67   Andrewe Nicholls ordered to pay Richd Conquest 338 lb tobo due as a balance on a bill.

p.67   "This Court takinge into consideracon the many debts which are
due out of the Estate of Thomas Tooker deceased, as alsoe lookinge uppon
the sad condicon of the Orphans of the said Tooker". The Sheriff is ordered to seize the estate, also what of right belongs to the relict of Tho
Tooker, by will of her former husband John Hatton deceased. Further that
Mr John Hill and Jno Smith divide Hatton's estate, according to his will,
betw the relict of Tooker and the said Hatton's children. Then the Sheriff
to deliver the share belonging to Tooker's widow to Lt Col Cornelius Loyd,
admr of said Tooker, and by him to be sold at Outory. Loyd to give in an
account.

p.67   Elizabeth Sibsey, widow and extrx of Capt Jno Sibsey, ordered to
pay Wm Jermy 1537 lb tobo due for Clerk's fees.

p.67   That at a Court held 15 Dec 1650, Guy Evans, Thomas Paxford, John
Eyre and Jane Latham, then servants to Mrs Anne Phillipps, widow, were
fined a hhd of tobo each for certain misdemeanors committed by them.
Considering "their poore Estate and condicon" the fines are remitted and
the original order voided.

p.67   On 15 Feb 1650/1 an order was granted Richd Conquest gent, agst
Edward Hall gent, for 569 lb tobo. On petition of Conquest the order is
revived.
Also an order agst Wm Hauthly for 245 lb tobo revived.

p.67   Certificate for 450 acres to Simond Overzee for importing
        Wm Andrewes   Margarett Sibble
        Darbye Kelly   Wm Hill
        Anne Breake   Theophilus Rogers
        Christian Christiance Addam Christiance
                Katheryne Eale

p.67   Certificate for 50 acres to John Finch for importing himself.

p.67   Certificate to Richd Joanes for 50 acres for importing John
Makefashion.

p.67   Certificate for 250 acres to John Smith for importing
        Himselfe   John Chase
        Anne Smith   Thomas Duke
        Gyles Smith

p.68   Certificate for 250 acres to Lemuell Mason gent for importing
               Robte Buckler   Phillipp Browne
               Tho Wilmot   and
               James Meccy   Blacke Jacke
These rights assigned to George Kempe.

p.68   Certificate for 150 acres to Christopher Rivers for importing
               Anne Jackson   Wm Morris
                    Thomas Morgan

p.68   Certificate for 300 acres to James Johnson for importing
               Margarett Guy   John Prescott
               Elizabeth Hughes   Richard Joanes
               Elizabeth Wimbleton   John Owens

p.68   A Court held 16 January 1653/4.
        Present
            Leift Coll Cornelius Loyd   Mr Lemuell Mason
            Major Thomas Lambert   Mr Francis Emperor
            Leift Coll John Sidney   Mr Thomas Bridge   Com'rs

p.68   Edw Robinson ordered to appear at next Court to answer suit of
John Piggott, merchant.

p.68   In regard "the poor Estate and condicon of Thomas Tooker an
Orphan and sonne of Thomas Tooker deceased", he is bound for 7 years to
Wm Vascombe to be taught the trade of cooper. A quaint entry.

p.68   In dif betw Robte Davis and Katheryne Dormer concerning the term
of years she has to serve, the cause ref to next Court. Mr Simond
Overzee to be there to testify.

p.68   Tho Addams subpened to this Court by Savill Gaskin to be paid 20
lb tobo for expense.

p.68   All differences betw Tho Edmonds and John Marshall referred to
hearing by Mr William Moseley and Leift Coll John Sidney on 10th Feb
next at the house of Mr Sidney.

p.68⁻ In dif betw Jno Baptist and Major Tho Lambert concerning time of
Baptist's service, Lambert appeals to the Genl Court. Mr Lemuell Mason
goes security for his appearance there.

p.68   Geo Raymond arrested Robte Davis to this Court and failed to
appear. He is nonsuited and ordered to pay Davis 50 lb tobo "for his
unjust molestacon".
Also Raymond arrested Tho Allen and did not appear. Is nonsuited and
ordered to pay Allen 50 lb tobo as above.

p.68   Jno Prescott ordered to pay Richd Joanes 549 lb tobo due him.
Also is ordered to pay Rd Joanes, as attorney for James Frisbye, mercht,
350 lb tobo due.

p.69   On petition of Edward Loyd, gent, Atty of Henery Catlin, regarding a tract of land, order that Mr Francis Emperor survey the land, and
that Mr John Hill, Thomas Wright, Richd Joanes and Robte Bowers be there
to assist him on the 30th or 31st of this January.

p.69   Raffe White ordered to pay Richd Joanes 838 lb tobo on 18 Feb next

p.69   Dif betw Mathewe Fassett, marriner, pltf, vs Major Tho Lambert
deft, appealed by Lambert to the Genl Court at James Citty.

p.69   Emanuell Delreere ordered to pay Tho Sherley 740 lb tobo due by
bill.

p.69   Certificate for 100 acres to Francis Fleetwood for importing
Margarett Fleetwood and Daniel Makefarsen.

p.69   Upon his petition, John Watford "beinge upwards of Sixty yeres
and past his labour" is henceforth free from taxes.

p.69   Dif betw Jno Godfrey, pltf, vs Tho Dadford, deft, to next Court.
That Edward Wilder be then and there present.

p.69   Dif betw Richd Conquest, gent, as assignee of Thomas Hewes, vs
Wm Haughley, regarding tobo and corn is referred to next Court.

p.69   Lt Col Cornelius Loyd, admr of Tho Tooker decd, ordered to pay
Gregory Parrett 320 lb tobo due him from the estate.

p.69   It was formerly ordered that Mr Tho Bridge have the tuition and
bringing up of Lemuell Phillipps, son of Mathew Phillipps, until he be
21. That Mary Smith, mother of the said Lemuell keeps him from Bridge.
Order that Mary Smith deliver the said Lemuell to the Sheriff on demand,
for the use of Mr. Bridge or pay him 8000 lb tobo.

p.69   Major Tho Lambert "for divers reasons and consideracons best
knowne to himselfe, protested agst Mathewe Fassett marriner for being
Maister of the Vessell called or knowne by the name of the Sea-horse,
according to former condi'con made betweene them".

p.69   Attachmt to Lt Col Cornelius Loyd for all tobo and corn in the
house of Edmund Bowman mercht belonging to Gregory Parrett for satisfaction of 3200 lb tobo and 7 bbl of corn due for servants wages and other
accounts

p.69   Dif betw Wm Merritt, pltf, vs Richd Conquest, gent, deft, upon
petition of Conquest is referred to next Court.

p.70   A former order of the Court to Christopher Rivers agst John
Lownes, gent, for 700 lb tobo cancelled in that Lownes says that Rivers
owes him more.

p.70   Attachmt to Major Lambert agst estate of Arthur Browne to cover
L 44. 16. 9 Sterling as appears by oath of Thos Allen "said Browne
beinge out of this Collony".

p.70   "Whereas Samuell Rutland hath in a most Scandelous manner abused
Mr Thomas Sayer". Rutland ordered to ask his forgiveness in open Court.

p.70   A former order that the Sheriff sell at Outcry the estate of Tho
Tooker decd, and deliver the same to Col Cornelius Loyd admr, to be held
until the next Court.

p.70   Attachmt to Tho Ivey agst so much of the estate belonging to the
wreck of Capt Luck's ship, in the hands of Richd Conquest, gent, to cover
2800 lb tobo due him by order of the Comm'rs for the wreck.
The same to Tho Bridge, gent, for 1200 lb tobo.

p.70   Certificate for 100 acres to Richd Joanes for importing Charles Hodges and Charles Wahab. (sic)

p.70   Attachmt to Tho Bridge, gent, who married the relict and admrx of Mathewe Phillipps decd, for 1400 lb tobo agst the estate of the wreck of Capt Lucke's ship in the hands of Mr Richd Conquest. This due Phillipps' widow.

p.70   Attachmt to Francis Emperor, gent, agst the est of Gerrard Cleaver for 335 lb tobo.
Also agst the est of Ciprian Mallard for 1200 lb tobo.
Robte Fitts acks judgt to Emperor for paymt of 745 lb tobo.

p.70   Attachmt to John Porter, senior, agst the estate of Derica (?) in hands of George Kempe for debts.

p.70   Attachmt to Major Tho Lambert agst the est of Geo Mee for 2674 lb tobo "the said Mee beinge out of this Collony".

p.70   Dif betw James Lopham pltf vs Lt Col Cornelius Loyd deft to next Court.

p.70   Dif betw Tho Goodrich, gent, pltf, vs John Prescott, deft, to next Court.

p.70   That Mr Edward Hall, chirurgeon, owes John Meekes, chirurgeon, 494 lb tobo. Hall to pay Tho Allen, Atty of Meekes. "Given under my hand this 13th day of January Ao Dm 1653" (1653/4)
                    Signed   Henr: Woodhouse

p.71   Ordered to be Recorded 16 January 1653/4.
Lancaster Lovett registers mark for cattle
John Martin   "
Henery Watson   "

p.71
Deed of Gift. Dated 3 April 1653. Recorded 16 Jan 1653/4. Henery Michells gives a cow and calf to Richard Whitehurst the younger, provided he lives till 21. If he die then the cattle to go to his brother James Whitehurst. If he die then the cattle to be divided amongst the rest of

the children of Richard Whitehurst.
Wit: Signed   Henery Michells
Edward Robinson
Thome x Elaxander
Delivered in presence of Francis Emperor.

p.71   Deed. 18 Oct 1651. Recorded 16 Jan 1653/4. Fransis Bright of
Elizabeth River in Co of Lower Norfolk, planter, sells John Laurence of
County of Nansimund, planter, for "one Horsemans Coate and two paire of
Shooes", already paid, 100 acres "which he holdeth from William Eyres of
Nansamond" which the said Eyes (sic) bought of Edward Selbye late of
Elizabeth River, on a Creek in Elizabeth River adj land of Richard
Jennings and being part of same patent by which Jennings' land is held,
etc. An interesting deed.
Wit: Signed   Francis x Bright
Jacob Seelley   John x Laurence
Walter x Grimes
-
John Laurence assigns above land to John Jallesse. 22 Jan 1652/3.
Wit: Signed   John x Laurence
Robte Locke
Recorded 25 Jan 1653/4.
-
John Jallesse assigns above to Rishd Jennings. 24 Jan 1653/4.
Wit: Signed   John x Jallesse
Tho: Goodrich
Will: Jermy

p.71   Recorded 25 Jan 1653/4.
"Darby Kelly aged about 26: yeres" swears he was in the cabin with Mr.
Overzee, who demanded of John Baptist how long he would serve. Baptist
said 5 years, and Overzee answered "it was enough".
Sworn 16 Jan 1653/4.   Signed   Darby Killy   (sic)

p.72   "Deposition of Francis Anketill about 28 yeres sworn and Examined".
Says he was aboard Mr Howes ship when Mathewe Fassett came aboard and
made an agreement in regard to transporting himself and his goods up to
Potuxon and was to give 1000 lb tobo when the goods were put aboard. Mr
Farmall being present and pretended he had power to command the boat,
"and with that requested this depon't to come into the said boate, and
being in they sett sayle and came ashoare neere the Ordinary". That the
evening after Major Lambert came aboard the vessel and took up of this
deponent goods to value of 1000 lb tobo in full of the freight to
Poyuxon.   Signed   Francis Anketill
Sworn 16 January 1653/4

p.72   "The deposition of Lemuell Mason gent aged 25: yeres or there
abouts". "Saith that Major Lambert beinge at his house when Danniell
Tanner was buried, havinge some discourse concerning the Cattle that
Mathewe Fassett had bought of this Depont:, the sd Major Lambert said,
that the said Fassett had noe power to buy nor barter for anything
without his consent, and further saith not"
Sworn 16 Jan 1653/4.   Signed   Lemuell Mason

p.72   "The deposition of John Martin aged about 37: yeres". Says that
Mathewe Fassett "about Six weeks before Christide" came to his house and
bought 20 hogs. About a month after he came with Major Lambert, "the
said Lambert seeminge not unwillinge at the sd Fassetts bargayne", desired this deponent to get up the hogs, saying they would send his mate
and some other seamen to kill them in 3 or 4 days.
Sworn 16 Jan 1653/4   Signed   John Martin

p.72   Robte Tillett, gent, has set up his name at the Court House "to
give notice of his intended voyage this Shipping for England according
to Act of Assembly".

p.72   Edward Loyd attests that "beinge in the house of Robte Evins on
the 28th of December last", in a room with Major Tho Lambert, Mathew
Fassett came and told Lambert "he had bought some biskett of one Mr
Rutherford at a pound and halfe". That Lambert was displeased and said
he could buy biscuit at York "for a hoggeshead a Butt".
Dated 10 Jan 1653/4.   Signed   Edd: Lloyd

p.72   Mathewe Fassett versus Major Tho: Lambert.
A Jury verdict in detail. The following is a short abstract.
(1) Mathewe Fassett as master and half owner of the ship has greater
     power than Major Lambert.
(2) That Fassett as master has full power to buy and sell "and in
     Shipping of William Hall for a marriner".
(3) That Lambert injured Fassett's credit by villifying him.
(4) That Fassett continue plans for his voyage, according to agreement
     with Lambert, without further interfereance.
(5) Lambert to pay Fassett 5000 lb tobo for injury to his character and
     credit here and abroad.
                            The Jurors
              Tho Sayer   Richard Joanes
              Henr: Barlowe   Tho: Allen
              Edmund Bowman   Gregory Parrett
              George Glane   Tho: Dadford
              Tho: Warde   John Pigott
              Rich: Lee   John Godfrey
This verdict presented in Court 16 Jan 1653/4.

p.73   "The deposition of Cap: William Atterbury aged about 47: yeres"
Says he heard Mr Christopher Coleman, Master of the Galleott say he
would attach 300 lb sugar in the hands of Thomas Morgin, one of the seamen, which sugar was due to Mr Maccomes for the passage of Thomas Allen's
kinswoman. That Allen had not paid the beef agreed upon for the passage
of his kinswoman, etc.   Signed   William Atterbury
Sworn 16 Jan 1653/4.

p.73   Ordered to be recorded 16 Jan 1653/4. Deed. A very long involved
entry. Dated 16 January 1653/4.   John Godfrey of Elizabeth River in the
County of Lower Norfolk, Boatwright, sells Thomas Dadford of Elizabeth
River, planter, 800 acres that Sir John Harvey, Governor, etc., granted
by patent, dated 26 July 1638, to John Gather.
       The land "being in the Lower County of Newe Norffolke" in the East-
ern Branch of Elizabeth River. Adjs Southerly upon the Eastern branch,
Easterly upon a creek called Dunn out of the Myre, Northerly and Westerly
into the woods, extending Easterly and Southerly beyond a point called
Oystershell Point.
       That the original patent was recorded in Nansemund Co 12 July 1649.
       That John Gater, with consent of Mary Gater his wife, assigned the
land to John Godfrey 12 July 1649.
Wit: Signed   Johis x Godfrey
Will: Jermy
Walter Huckstepp

p.74   A Court held 15 Feb 1653/4.
       Present
             Leift Coll Cornelius Loyd   Mr Francis Emperor
             Major Thomas Lambert   Mr Thomas Bridge
             Mr Lemuell Mason   Mr Thomas Goodrich
             Mr William Moseley.   Com'rs

p.74   Certificate for 300 acres to Tho Greene for importing
             Jane Harvey   William Scott
             Thomas Harvey   James Bradshawe
             John Haule   Thomas Browne

p.74   That Christopher Burrowes, gent, decd, owed, in his lifetime, 400
lb tobo to Tho Woodward, now assigned to Jno Holmes. Order that William
Smith, who married Mary Burrowes the relict and extrx, settle the a/c.

p.74   Moyses Linton to pay debt of 829 lb tobo due Tho. Daynes.
Also Richd Becke to pay debt of 340 lb tobo due Tho Daynes

p.74   Dif in accounts betw Tho Daynes and Tho Edmonds are referred to
a full hearing before Major Tho Lambert, Mr Tho Goodrich, Mr Tho Sayer
and Wm Jermy, on Wednesday next, the 22 of this Feb, at the house of the
said Mr Tho Daynes. Order that Daynes and Edmonds bind themselves in the
sum of 10000 lb tobo to abide by the award.

p.74   Dif betw Robte Darby, pltf, and Ciprian Mallard, deft, referred
to next Court.

p.74   In dif betw Jno Marshall pltf and Tho Edmonds deft, Edmonds to
pay Marshall 100 lb tobo for a canoe.

p.74.   The following referred to next Court.
Wm Daynes, atty of Jno Jasperson, pltf, vs Peter Malborne, deft.
Richd Woster vs Moyses Linton.

p.74   Tho Daynes, gent, to pay debt of 160 lb tobo due Jane Wood.

p.74   That Tho Daynes, gent, "hath in a most contemptuous manner
slited and disobeyed a warrent made against him by Mr Emperor one of
the Com'rs This Court takinge it into consideracon the grand abuse
thereof", Daynes is fined 300 lb tobo.

p.74   Dif betw Katheryne Dormer, pltf, vs Robte Davis, deft, to next
Court, Mr Simond Overzee to be present.

p.74   Dif betw Jno Pigott, pltf, and Edwd Robinson, deft, to next Court.

p.74   In dif betw John Lownes, pltf, vs Xpofer Rivers, deft, concerning
"certeyne scandelous words spake by the said Rivers", Rivers to pay 100
lb tobo to Lownes.

p.74   In dif betw Jno Lownes, pltf, vs Xpofer Rivers, deft, regarding
a man servant, upon verdict of a jury, Lownes appeals to the Genl Court.

p.75   Dif betw Jno Godfrey pltf vs Tho Dadford deft ref to next Court.

p.75   Robte Powes arrested at suit of Richard Conquest, gent, on behalf
of Thos Tooker, gent, fails to appear. The Sheriff to produce him at next
Court.

p.75   Attachmt to Richd Conquest, gent, agst est of Bartholomew Renoh
for 700 lb tobo.

p.75   Mathewe Fassett arrested at suit of Major Tho Lambert failed to
appear. Laurence Phillipps who went his bond (bail) to produce him at
next Court.

p.75   Dif betw Lt Col Cornelius Loyd, pltf, vs Gregory Parrett, deft,
to next Court.

p.75   Robte Mackrery bound by Indenture to Wm Wilson for term of 8 years,
being dated 10 March 1651/2 and Mackrery having changed the Indenture
"by unjust meanes" to serve full term.

p.75   In dif betw Jno Baptist, pltf, vs Major Tho Lambert, deft, regarding term of Baptist's service, and Lambert having appealed to the Genl
Court, Baptist to have a week's time free to himself to prepare his
testimony.

p.75   That there was the last Court an order agst Mary Smith, widow, at
suit of Tho Bridge, gent. She having since married John Turner the order
is renewed agst him.

p.75   The next Court 22nd March.

p.75   Recorded 15 Feb 1653/4.   Power of Atty. Dated 12 Feb 1653/4.
Savill Gaskin of the parish of Lynhaven in the County of Lower Norfolk,
planter, to "my welbeloved frend Mathewe Fassett Marriner" to demand of
William Higgumbothum a bill of 1100 lb tobo.
Wit: Signed   Savill Gaskin
Edward Hall Chirurgeon
Jacobi x Lopham

p.75   Recorded 15 Feb 1653/4.   Power of Atty. Dated 29 Apl 1652. John
Jasperson to "my welbeloved frend William Daynes" to collect debts "with-
in the Capes of Virginia".
Wit: Signed   Jan: Jaspers'   (sic)
Katheryne Cooper
Allexander x Rogers

p.75   Recorded 15 Feb 1653/4. Receipt. Dated 15 Feb 1653/4. Wm Hall
to John Holmes for a heifer. "Due from said Holmes unto an Orphan of John
Sutton Deceased named Francis and now under the tui'con of William
Haughle", which heifer was given to said Francis Sutton by Mr Richard
Conquest.   Signed   Will   x   Hall
Wit: Thomas Warde

Note: This method of spelling our good old name of Hall is right much
for my digestion.   B.F.

p.76   Recorded 15 Feb 1653/4.   Bond. Dated 16 Jan 1652/3. Bartholomew
Hoskins of Elizabeth River in Co of L. N. to secure sale of 600 acres to
John Greene of Chuckatucke in Co of Upper Norfolk. This 600 acres "Lyenge
in Rapuhannocke River on the south side joyninge upon Clement Thrush".
Wit: Thomas Bridge   Signed   Bartho Hoskins

p.76   Recorded 15 Feb 1653/4. Deed. Dated 6 Feb 1653/4. Savill Gaskin,
planter, of Lynhaven parish in Co of L. N., sells Thos Moore, for 2000
lb tobo, 80 acres in Lynhaven parish, lately patented. Land bounded by
Davis South Southeast and by Burrowes Northwest.
Wit: William Warde   Signed   Savill Gaskin

p.76   Recorded 15 Feb 1653/4. Will of Thomas Godbye of Elizabeth River
in Co of Lower Norfolk. Dated 8 April 1652. This will apparently record-
ed at Godby's request while he was still living.
To wife Anne all estate, she sole exor.
Wit: Tho Tooker   Signed   Thomas   x   Godbye
        Lewis Fundermull
Postscript:
To wife's sister Elizabeth Bearre a cow.
Wit: 10th Feb 1653/4   Signed   Thomas   x   Godbye
Rich: Lee

p.76   Ordered to be Recorded 15 Feb 1653/4.   In dif betw John Lownes
vs Xpofer Rivers concerning a servant the Jury find for the deft, and
the pltf to be dismissed with costs of suit.
                             Jurors
            Thomas Daynes   John Carraway
            Edmund Bowman   Will: Wilson
            John Godfrey   John Workman
            Thomas Warde   Richard Largrane
            Will Robinson   Tho: Greene
            Richd Whitehurst   Richard Sternall

p.77   Recorded 16 March 1653/4. Deed of Gift. Dated 1 July 1653. John

Rabley of the Newe Pocoson in the County of Yorke; Virginia, gives all
his property to his 3 children, John Rabley Junior, Thomas Rabley and
Elizabeth Rabley, to be delivered to them when they are 21.
Wit: Signed   John x Rabley
Wm Hill
Thomas x Oxley

p.77   Recorded 24 March 1653/4. Agreement, dated 23 March 1653/4 betw
Simond Overzee and Francis Land concerning a ship. Arbitrated by Lt Col
Jno Sidney and Francis Emperor.
Wit: Signed   Simond Overzee
John Sidney   Francis Land
Francis Emperor

p.77   Recorded 22 March 1653/4.
Inventory of James Starling, dec'd, taken 20 Feb 1653/4.
Covers an entire page and includes:
1   cros saw lent William Smith
1   draweing knife lent to James Phillipps
1   bill of Willyam Cleavers
Cattell left in hands of me James Lopham
Test   Signed   James Lopham
Savill Gaskin
Willyam Ward
An addl inventory was sworn to by Lopham 18 April 1654.

p.78   Recorded 22 March 1653/4. Bond. Dated 16 Nov 1653. James Steward
and Owen Hayes, 2000 lb tobo, to John Macey. The condition of this bond
being that James Steward and his wife behave themselves properly to John
Macey and his wife.   Signed   James x Steward
Wit: Owen x Hayes
Andrew x Bodnam   (?)
Willyam Blake

p.78   Recorded 22 March 1653/4. An account "of what is due from James
Starlinge to me Lank: Lovett for his lyenge sicke at my house 5 weekes
the last som'er". Then follows an interesting list of funeral expenses,
etc.

p.78   Recorded 22 March 1653/4.
Receipt. Dated 25 August 1653. "Received by me Stephen Hamlin from James
Thelaball for the use of Lemuell Mason" 1000 lb tobo in full of all a/cs
between Capt Abraham Reade and said Mason.
Wit: Signed   Stephen Hamlin
Thomas Pirson

p.78   Recorded 22 March 1653/4.
Deed. Dated 15 Nov 1653. "John Baker of Lynhaven parish in the County of
Lower Norfolke in the Country of Virginia singleman, sonne and heire
appearent of John Baker late of the parish St Martins in the feilds in
the County of Middlesex nere London in England late Deceased" sells
Francis Land of Lynhaven parish in the Co of Lower Norfolk, all estate
"within the Commonwealth of England . . . and beinge within the parish
of St Martins in the feilds in the County of Middlesex". All goods late
in "possession of Elizabeth Baker widd' my mother Deceased". This is a
long entry. It is possible that the name may be Saker rather than Baker
in that the capital B looks remarkably like an S.
Wit: Signed   John Baker
Edward Cannon
John Johnsons mark
Simon Barrowes

p.79   Recorded 22 March 1653/4. Gregory Parrett assigns to Thos Daynes
a cow and 2 calves to guarantee paymt of 1049 lb tobo. Dated 16th Feb
1652/3.   Signed   Gregory Parrett
Wit:
Will Daynes
Johis x Marshall

p.79   At a Quarter Court held at James Citty the 14th of March 1653.
        Present   Rich: Bennett Esq'r Governor
                        Coll William Claybourn   Coll Ludlow
                        Coll Thomas Battus (Pettus)   Coll Higinson
                        Leift Coll Freeman   Col Wm Taylor
Note: This list of the Council is badly written. B.F.

p.79   Mr Francis Emperor appointed High Sheriff of Lower Norfolk Co.
                                Test Rob't Huberd, Clk Conseld

p.79   Recorded 22 March 1653/4.   A long letter dated "In Yarmoth the
6th December 1653" from William Scapes to Capt Thomas Willoughby, Mr
Lemuell Mason and Mr John Holmes in Virginia, concerning tobacco rec'd
for a/c of Henery Seawell.

p.80   Recorded 25 March 1653/4.   Deed. Dated 28 Oct 1652. Richd Foster
sells Wm Warde 50 acres in Bennetts Creek and adj SW on land which did
belong to William Est and now belongs to John Stratton the son of John
Stratton, and is part of land belonging to James Starling.
Wit: Signed   Richard x Foster
James Starling

p.80   Lt Col Cornelius Loyd discharges Wm Capps of 900 lb tobo, part of a bill due Sir Wm Berkeley concerning the ship wreck of Mr Lucke.
Dated 29 March 1653.
Wit: Edward Robinson   Signed   Cornelius Loyd
Recorded 1 April 1654.

p.80   A Court held 22 March 1653/4
       Present
           Coll Francis Yardley   Leift Coll John Sidney
           Leift Coll Cor'ls Loyd   mr Lemuell Mason
           mr Henery Woodhouse   mr Francis Emperor
           Major Thomas Lambert   mr Thomas Bridge   Com'rs

p.80   Letters of admr to Francis Emperor, gent, on est of Robt Fitts, deceased, as greatest creditor.

p.80   Letters of admr to James Lopham on est of Jas Starlinge, deceased, as greatest creditor, with consent of Lancaster Lovett another creditor.

p.80   Jas Lopham, admr of Jas Starling, decd, to pay Lancaster Lovett 1600 lb tobo due for expense during Starling's sickness.
Also to pay the following debts due from the estate:
       John Martin   1292 lb tobo
       Lopham, his expense
       Francis Land   491   "
       Geo Wright   300   "
       Lawrence Phillipps   470   "

p.80   Ciprian Marriott ordered to pay Robte Darby 630 lb tobo due him.

p.81   In dif betw John Godfrey pltf vs Edward Wilder deft, Wilder is ordered to begin to build a corn house 30 x 20 feet before the 20 April according to agreement. Tho Dadford stood engaged for Wilder, etc.

p.81   Dif betw Richd Sternell pltf vs Tho Godbye deft dismissed, "and not to be brought any more to this board".

p.81   Edw Robinson Chirurgeon ordered to pay debt of 342 lb tobo due John Piggott, mercht.
Also Piggott to pay Robinson 120 lb tobo due him.

term she has to serve, she to serve her full term of 7 years.

p.82   Dif betw Richd Woster and Moyses Linton referred to next Court.

p.82   "for some speciall reasons" the Sheriff to "take into safe custody
the boddy of Andrew Nicholls and him to deteyne untill further Order".

p.82   Capt Tho. Willoughby, Mr Lemuell Mason and John Holmes to accept
proposition of Mr William Scapes concerning the taking of Henery Sewell
an Orphan as an apprentice, according to a letter produced.

p.82   In dif betw Richd Conquest, gent, vs William Haughly, Haughly to
pay Conquest,as assignee of Tho Hewes, 247 lb tobo with 5 yrs forbearance.

p.82   Henery Snayle ordered to pay Col Francis Yardley 578 lb tobo.

p.82   "For speciall reasons and consideracons manifested to this Court:
It is Ordered that Wm Hattersley build sufficiently one Duckinge or
Cookinge stoole in some convenient place in the little Creeke in the
parish of Lynhaven, and to be done by the next Court".

Note: I don't quite understand what the 'Cookinge' has got to do with
it. It is to be hoped the word was passed to Mrs. Heigham that this
business was going forward, which was done no doubt.   B.F.

p.82   In Aug 1652 Tho Hall obtained an order agst Robert Powes Atty of
Francis Land. This order revived.

p.82   Lt Col Cornelius Loyd, Atty of Richd Chapman who is out of the
Colony, is ordered to pay 200 lb tobo to Wm Jermy for a case of Drams
loaned by Jermy to Chapman.

p.82   The exor (name not shown in original record) of Jno Moore the
Surveyor, to pay 200 lb tobo to Laurence Phillipps, due him in Moore's
lifetime.

p.82   By order of the Governor and Council, dated 14 March 1653/4. Mr
Francis Emperor was sworn High Sheriff of Lower Norfolk County.

1653/4
1654

p.82   Certificate for 100 acres to Lancaster Lovett for importing
                Archbell Hunter   Gabriell Johnston

p.83   Recorded 16 Apl 1654.   Thomas Willett, merchant, of Newe Plimmouth
in Newe England, sells Mr Mathewe Fassett all interest in the "Barque
commonly called the Hopewell". 26 tons. Dated 20 Oct 1652 "now in Newe
Amsterdam in New Netherlands".
Wit: Signed   Tho Willett
Olessd Stearse
George Barker

p.83   Recorded 16 Apl 1654.   Major Tho Lambert acquitts Mathew Fassett
from all debts. "and alsoe that the Barque called the Seahorse, and all
that is in her, fitted for the Barbadoes, doth rightly belonge to the
said Fassett". Dated 10 April 1654.
Wit: Signed   Thomas Lambert
Walter Huckstep   his: x: marke

Postscript: Also Tho Lambert acknowledges to pay half of 1000 lb tobo
to Col Burbage due him by bill, and half of 1800 lb tobo due to Mr Richardson. Dated 10 Apl 1654.

p.83   A Court held 18 April 1654.
        Present
                Coll Francis Yardley   Mr William Moseley
                Leift Coll Cornelius Loyd   Mr Thomas Bridge
                Major Thomas Lambert   Mr William Daynes
                Leift Collo John Sidney   Com'rs

p.83   Judgt ack by John Taylor to Thos Manninge, gent, Atty of Segar de
Hem, for 1336 lb tobo, and assigned over in open Court to Henery Bastard,
merchant.

p.83   Certificate for 200 acres to Moyses Linton for importing
                Pennellope Gilbert   Dorothy Bright
                John Bradshawe   Augustus Addison

p.83   An involved entry concerning a difference betw Tho Daynes, gent,
and Capt George Raymond, regarding tobo to be pd for sugar. This appeal-
to the Genl Court. Wm Edwards is Atty of Raymond. Thomas Goodrich goes
security for Edwards.

p.83. The wife (her name not shown in the original record) of
Laurence Plummer, dec'd, to have letters of admr on est of her late
husband, and to pay Simond Overzee 4500 lb tobo due from the estate.

p.83 Deborah Heigham, wife of Geo Heigham "hath in a most scandelous
manner abused Sarah the wife of John Godfrey". She is ordered to ask her
pardon on her knees in Court and pay 2000 lb tobo for use of the County.

p.84 Dif betw Tho Hall, cooper, vs Francis Land to be settled at next
Court.

p.84 Elizabeth Sibsey, widow and extrx of Capt Jno Sibsey, ordered to
pay 1790 lb tobo due from the estate to Richd Pinner, Atty of Stephen
Gearey.

p.84 Alice Spencer "hath in a most scandelizinge manner abused the wife
of Coll: Francis Yardley". She is ordered to go to the house of Colonel
Yardley and ask forgiveness.

p.84 Lt Col John Sidney, Mr Tho Bridge, Lancaster Lovett and Robte
Powes to divide the estate of Christopher Burroughs decd betw the widow
and orphans on 20 May next at the house of Wm Smith who married the widow.

p.84 The fine of 2000 lb tobo agst Deborah Heigham remitted, She ack
her abuse of Sarah Godfrey and submitting hersef.

p.84 Certificate for 200 acres to Richd Whitehurst for importing
        Allexander Rose   Downgh Gomogh   (?)
        Daniell Maswille   Margarett Souleman

p.84 The relict (name not shown) of Gregory Parrett, decd, to take
letters of admr on the estate and pay "a great some of tobacco and corne"
due Lt Col Cornelius Loyd for servants wages.

. . . .

Note: Perhaps this is enough of the Lower Norfolk records for the time
being. I have notes for future volumes if I have strength to produce
them.   Beverley Fleet.

INDEX

Ackton, Richard 70. 71
Addams, Thomas 26. 80
Addeson, Augustine 27
Addison, Augustus 94
Alexander, Thos 16. 84
Allen, Thos. 31. 46. 48. 54. 72
        76. 77. 78. 81. 82. 83
        85. 86
Andrewes, Thos. 78
        Wm. 79
Anketill, Fr: 84
Anthony, Wm. 65
Ashall, Geo. 26. 34
Ashton, Peeter 77
Atterbury, Wm. 86. 92
Attkinson, Robt. 9. 23. 51
        Thos. 34
Avrill, Rd. 69. 77

Bacon, Mr. 45
Baker, John Jr. John Sr. and
        Elizabeth 91
Banden, Peter 56
Banks, John 34
Baptist, John 12. 81. 84. 88
        (You would think any
        Christian gentleman
        would hesitate to keep
        any such person in
        servitude)
Barkelett, Leift: 75
Barker, Geo. 94
Barlowe, Henry 27. 37. 85
Barnard, Wm 18
Barnes, Edward 93
Barnester, Peeter 15
Barrnes, Peter 23. 24
Barrowe, Simond 13. 91
Basnett, Wm 28
Bastard, Henry 94
Batty, Ferdinando 72. 73
Bearré, Eliz: 89   —
Becké, Richd. —50. 86
Bell, Alex: 56
        John 56
Bellamy, Adam 6. 9
Bemiss see Beymus
Benoe, Wm. 21

Bennett, Mary 56
        Governor Richard 28. 42. 91
        Robert 70
        Samuel 19
        William 69
Berkeley, Sir William 18. 19. 40. 66
                68. 76. 92
        His letters, note, 75
Beymus, John Jr and Sr. 38
Bigge, Jno. 37
        John and Johan 43
Biggs, Jno. 29
Bisley, Geo. 68
Bitoge, Richard 18
Black Jack, a slave. 53. 60. 80
Blacké, Anne 56
Blake, Wm 90—
Blunt, John 61
Bodnam, Andrew 90
Bonner, Cornelius 33
Booker, Edwd. 76. 77
Bosworth, Mr. 47
Bowers, Robt. —27. 38. 52. 57. 58. 81
Bowles, John 69
Bowman, Edmund 49. 55. 58. 60. 66.
                70. 82. 85. 89
Bowsey, John 71
Bradshawe, James 86
        Jno. 94
Brakes, Henry 8. 10. 13. 58. 67
Bray, Plummer (?) 59
Breake, Anne 79
Brewster, Sack: 73
Brice, Mr. 14. 36
        Judith 37
        Robt. 37
        William 93
Bridge, Thomas 7. 9. 21. 27. 29. 37
        40. 42. 45. 47. 50. 60. 62
        63. 64. 65. 73. 74. 82. 83
        88. 89. 95
        As Com'r. 15. 21. 25. 26
        28. 32. 33. 41. 44. 46. 47
        48. 52. 58. 61. 63. 66. 68
        75. 76. 80. 86. 92. 94
Bright, Dorothy 94
        Francis 84
Brooke, John 59

Fowler, (Will), Robt Jr and Sr.
   Mary and George 60
Fowler, Robt and Mary 53. 58. 67
     Robt Jr and Sr. 78
Freeman, Adjutant 18
     Lt Col 91—
     Nicholas 63
Fripps, Jno 73
Frisbye, Jas 33. 35. 81
Fulcher, Tho. 67
Fundermull, Lewis 89

Gardner, Rd. 66
Garnitant, Peter 32. 42
Garrett's house 45
Gaskin, Ann 72
     Savill 6. 9. 51. 57. 66
       70. 72. 80. 88. 89. 90
Gather, (Gater), Jno and Mary 86
Gay, Geo: 17
Gearey, Stephen 45. 93. 95
Gibbs, Nathaniel 61
Gilbert, Penellope 94
Gilham, Jno. 6. 8. 9. 13
     Jno Jr. and Sr. 5
Gwen, Griffin 67
Glane, Geo 70. 76. 85
     Geo Jr and Sr and Mary 64
     Geo Jr and Sr 63
Glaskock, Robt 50
Godby, Anne 29. 89
     Tho 37. 50. 62. 66. 69
       70. 92
     Tho and Anne 89
Godfrey, Gyles 69
     John 37. 52. 59. 66. 70
       81. 85. 86. 87. 89
       92
     Jno and Sarah 95
Godwyn, Tho 31
Gomogh, Donngh (?) 95
Goodrich, Anne 43
     Thomas 5. 13. 35. 42.
       43. 49. 61. 72. 73. 83
       84. 87. 94
       As Com'r: 15. 21. 26.
       28. 41. 45. 48. 52. 61
       63. 76. 86
Goodwin, Tho. (?) This name
     apparently in error 68
Gookin, Jno. 23
     Mrs Sarah 25

Gore, John 56
Gosden, George 5. 35
Gouldsmith, Mary 35. 58
Gradwell, Edw: 10. 13
Grantor, Peter —37
Greene, John 56. 89
     Thos. 27. 56. 78. 86. 89
Gregman, Jno. 34
Gregory, Tho. 59
Griffen, Wm. 59
Griffith, Edw: 66
Grimes, Robt: 32. 50. 70
     Walter 57. 58. 84
Grintoe, Peter 44
Gunnell, Mr. 65
     Edward 45
Gutter, Mary 33
Guy, Margaret 80
Gwinn, Alex: 37

Hall, Mr. 68
     Edward 10. 21. 25. 26. 30.
       44. 47. 61. 65. 66. 77.
       79. 83. 88. 93
     Edward, Sr. 42
Haule, John 86
Hall, Thomas 8. 10. 11. 17. 20. 24
       25. 37. 47. 72. 74. 93
       95
     William (also as Haughle) 56
       85. 89
Halsey, Henry 65
Ham, Jeremy 41
Hamlin, Stephen 90
Hancocke, Mathew 56
     Sarah 18
     Simon 7. 14. 17. 19. 36
       75
Hargrave, Richd. 51
Harlowe, Richd 55
Harris, John 34
     William and Co. 30
Harryes Necke 22
Harvey, Jane and Thomas 86
     Sir John 57. 86
     Thomas 93
Hattersley, Wm 60. 71. 93
     Wm and Margaret 48. 66
     Wm and Mary (?) 63
Hatton, John 34. 79
     Thomas 51. 52
Hatton's estate 62

        (Good God ! I'd hardly expected
        to find origins of style in
        Lower Norfolk. Can this be a
        sample of Virginia boasts ? B.F.

Makey, Danl 61
Malborne, Peter 87
Mallard, Ciprian 83. 87
Manning, John 53
          Thos. 94
Marrington, Marmaduke 56
Marriott, Ciprian 92
Marsh, Tho: 21. 33. 34. 50. 51
          52
Marshall, John 49. 80. 87. 91
Martin, John 16. 26. 33. 35. 38
          41. 42. 46. 50. 59
          64. 72. 74. 83. 85
          92
Mason, Alice 5
      Anne 60. 76
      Francis 5. 9
      Lemuell 5. 8. 9. 12. 16
          21. 22. 23. 35. 36. 41.
          44. 48. 58. 60. 63. 62.
          65. 70. 72. 74. 76. 77.
          78. 80. 81. 90. 91. 93.
          Deposition 85
          As Com'r: 6. 7. 12. 15.
          21. 26. 28. 33. 35. 41.
          48. 52. 58. 61. 63. 68.
          76. 80. 86. 92
      Mrs. Mary 67
      Nicholas 13. 60. 67. 78
      Trusteram 12. 24
Maston, Anne 64
Maswille, Danl 95
Mathewes, Col Saml 18
          Tobias 45. 46. 55
Mathias, Mathew 71
May, Jno. (his orphans) 29
Mc-Allister, Alex: 42
Make Allestre, Allexander 42. 56
McLeod see Macklude 46
Meares, Mr. 47
          John 70
Mecoy, James 80
Mee prob also as Migh
Mee, Geo: 35. 83
Meekes, Jno. 83
Mendham, Jno. 16. 36. 67
Merritt also as Marriott
Merritt, Geo: 72. 73
          Henry 10. 17. 69
          William 33. 43. 82
Michells, Andrew 36

Michells, Henry 83. 84
Migh prob also as Mee
Migh, Geo: 9. 10. 11. 16. 21
Milicent, James 56
Miller, James 59
        John 55
Mograth, Charles 33
Moodye, Robt (prob Woody) 55
Moore, - 48
Moore, John a - I think meaning a Moor
          named John. 70   B.F.
Moore, John 93
        Thomas 89
        William 44. 64
Morgan, Morgin, etc.
Morgan, Charles 38
        Isaac 23. 48
        Lewis 55
        Owen 72   (Morgin)
        Rouland 8. 11. 12. 32. 37
        Thos: 69. 76. 77. 80. 86
Morris, William 80
Moseley, Mrs. Susan 30. 31
        William 14. 17. 19. 21. 22.
          30. 33. 34. 35. 36. 71. 73
          As Com'r: 15. 21. 26. 28
          63. 68. 80. 86. 94
          Jewels and letter 30. 31
Muckeallen, John 56

Nansemond Co. 2. 84. 86
Neale, Robt: 93
Needham, Henry 67
Needham's Marsh 19
Nelson (?), Andrew 56
New England 15. 94
New Norfolk County 2
Newman, Jno: 53. 67
        Thomas 36
Nicholls, Andrew 21. 26. 68. 78. 93
          Richard 57
Norfolk County origin 2
          records 3. 4
Norwood, Mr. 67

Odeon, Mr. 47
Onthery, James 18
Orpdrood (?) Richard 70
Orphans Court 46. 70
Outkery (?), James 17
Overzee, Simond, (see next page)

Once again we come to an end. Not a sure finish,
for there is error in these Abstracts. If you do
not know it — then I do.   B.F.